Organizational

Aloumedjo Zam Thierry Farrel

Organizational Chart and Professional Efficiency

Restructuration of the Cameroon Customs Administration

LAP LAMBERT Academic Publishing

Publisher:
LAP LAMBERT Academic Publishing
is a trademark of
International Book Market Service Ltd., member of OmniScriptum Publishing Group
17 Meldrum Street, Beau Bassin 71504, Mauritius

Printed at: see last page
ISBN: 978-613-9-45219-4

ORGANIZATIONAL CHART AND PROFESSIONAL EFFICIENCY

RESTRUCTURING THE CAMEROON CUSTOMS ADMINISTRATION

1ST edition

Dr ALOUMEDJO ZAM Thierry Farrel

i

ORGANIZATIONAL CHART AND PROFESSIONAL EFFICIENCY

RESTRUCTURING THE CAMEROON CUSTOMS ADMINISTRATION

To the Lord God Almighty, for his love and grace in my humble life and family

ACKNOWLEDGEMENT

My sincere gratitude goes to all those without exception who contributed in the writing and publishing of this research work, especially my family

ABSTRACT

The aim of this research work is to explore the connection between organizational chart and organizational performance in order to propose a restructuration of the Cameroon Customs administration. Much has been written about these concepts separately, but there is not enough integrated conceptual framework available for the combination of the said concepts, especially in a sub-Saharan public fiscal administration, whereby the goal here is to develop such a framework. We do this in a number of steps, starting with a presentation of the existing approaches, models, theories with respect to organizational chart and organizational performance. This is followed by a search for the linkage between the two concepts or variables, as a starting point for an integrated model and an in-depth case study regarding the Cameroon Customs department. I continue with a research methodology based on a mixed approach i.e. qualitative and quantitative data collection and treatment tools in order to address efficiently the research problem. I conclude with the presentation of recommendations and suggestions for further research. Statistical tests did indicate significant differences between the performance of firms based on the preciseness and quality of their organization or charts. There are indications of possible positive change in performance after the initiation of more precise, clear and restructured organizational chart for the Customs administration, relatively both to users and non-users of such systems.

Key words: Organizational chart, efficiency, Cameroon customs administration

LIST OF ABBREVIATIONS

- ASP: Assistant regional director in charge of personnel and administrative affairs
- ASC: Assistant regional director in charge of commercial operations
- ASS: Assistant regional director in charge of surveillance
- ASP: Assistant regional director in charge of statistics and performance
- CCA: Cameroon customs administration
- CCFU: customs central funds unit
- DGD1: inspection of services
- DGD2: division of customs investigation and surveillance
- DGD3: legislation and litigations
- DGD4: IT division
- DGD5: Directorate of resource and logistics
- DGD6: Division of finance, external trade and currency exchange controls
- DGD7: Division of statistics and recovery
- DGD8: Division of studies, trade facilitation and risks management
- DGD9: Division of international cooperation and tax bases
- DGD10: Customs intervention Special group
- DGD11: Customs training center
- DRH: Director of human resource
- DAP: Director of supplies and real estates management
- DSD: Director of customs surveillance
- DED: Director of customs investigations
- DCI: Director of internal audit and control
- DAJ: Director of legal affairs and litigations
- DEF: Director of studies, trade facilitation and international cooperation
- DSR: Director of statistics and recovery
- DIR: Director of IT, networking and risk management
- GMC: General manager of customs
- MINFI: Ministry of finance
- RD: Regional director
- SD: Sub directorates
- SU: Sub units
- SDC: Sub director of mails management and translation
- SDI: Sub director of communication, information and public relations
- SIC: service of information and communication
- MS: Mailing service

LIST OF TABLES AND FIGURES

- Table 1: overlapping skills of the strategic units
- Table 2: The personnel of the CCA from 2010 to 2016
- Table 3: Correlations between organization chart;
- Workforce planning and organizational performance
- Table 4: The civil branch of the CCA
- Table 5: Interviews

OUTLINE

INTRODUCTION

Nowadays most organizations are designed on the basis of an organizational chart. However the structuring does not always presents all guaranties in terms of efficiency. To take the example of sub-Saharan African countries, especially Cameroon, it is possible to observe that despite the presence of charts, many public administrations face the issues of overlapping skills and conflicts relating to it among the various units, departments or even ministries. This is more true in the Cameroon public administration where we can register 100% overlaps among the 12 directorates of the said organization. The situation is observable inside the ministry of finance where the customs department overlaps skills with some structures like the treasury and the taxation on certain domains and with external structures like the financial investigations unit or the ministry of trade. This most often impact negatively on the performance of the organizations.

At first sight the concept of organizational chart seems to be closely connected with organizational performance. Organizational structure has been the subject of some reviews (cunnings and Berger, 1976); (Ford and Slocum, 1977) or (Scott, 1976); etc. However the correlation in between the previous concept and its impact on organizational performance seems not to have been sufficiently explored especially as the Customs department is concerned.

Among the few who studied the topic, we can refer to Dan R Dalton and al in organizational structure and performance: a critical review, Academy of management review, 1980, vol 5, N°1, P.49-64. It is stated in the said works that the link in between the two may appear obvious notwithstanding the insufficiency of literature in the domain and the ambiguity of the results of the said literature. The performance and capacity to innovate from one organization to the other may differ according to the organization structure (A Cosh, X Fu, A Hughes, Small Business Economics, Springer, 2012). Organization structure and management style's influence and impact can be measures on organizational effectiveness (P Lansley, P Sadler, T Webb - Omega, 1974 – Elsevier). According to Child, J. (1972), Organizational structure, environment and performance are inter-related. Structure and financial performance is

1

correlated (DL Rhoades, PL Rechner, 2001). For Bat Batjargal (2003), relational embeddedness and resource embeddedness have direct positive impacts on firm performance, whereas structural embeddedness has no direct impacts on performance.

Until recently, less attention was given to the organization of the Customs department in HRM literature and practice in the Cameroon Customs administration, but the interest now seems to be growing fast with the intervention and pressure of stakeholders such as the World Bank Group and the World Customs Organization relating to the efficiency of the Customs department. The link in between the two aforementioned concepts is of main interest for us, as we ask our self the question whether a restructured organization will influence positively the efficiency of the Customs department. Through a concurrent triangulation design that implies converging both quantitative and qualitative data in order to better understand and answer research questions (Martens 2001), I will be able to test the research hypothesis of our work i.e. structure organization has a positive and direct impact on individual and collective performance.

The benefits of this research can be identified in the theoretical, methodological and managerial domains. Theoretically the structure organization theories and concepts explored led us to the fact that well elaborated organizational chart are useful for any organization that looks for performance and effective organizational culture. Methodologically the research work tried to mix both qualitative and quantitative analyses in order to better understand and answer the research problem. It further extended the scope of scientific methods explored in a study as it involved interviews; questionnaires; Performance tests; observations; follow up focus groups and document analysis. In managerial terms it puts at the disposal of managers in general and the customs administration of Cameroon in particular, tools to better up their organizational performance and job satisfaction in a context marked by competitiveness and globalization.

The present research work comprises three main parts which are first the conceptual and theoretical frameworks; secondly the methodological approach and thirdly conclusions and contributions of the research.

PART I: CONCEPTUAL AND THEORETICAL FRAMEWORKS

A literature review is defined as a search and evaluation of the available literature in a given subject or chosen topic area. It documents the state of the art with respect to the subject or topic you are writing about. It surveys, synthesizes, critically analyses the literature in a chosen area. Our literature review will focus on the concepts of organizational chart and efficiency.

CHAPTER I: LITTERATURE REVIEW

SECTION I: ORGANIZATIONAL CHART

The concept of organizational chart is made up of 02 key terms which are: "organization" and "Chart". The first term derives from Latin « organum » and from Greek « organon » referring to the act of structuring, delimitating, and articulating harmoniously in a way that is pleasant and efficient, as it must be stated the origins of organization come from musical organs. The second one "chart" originates from Latin "charta" meaning map, card or paper in reference to «map for the use of navigators". From etymologies, it is therefore possible to infer the definition of organizational chart as the map guiding the smooth running and structuring of an institution or body with the aim of attaining a specific objective. Organizational structure is typically a hierarchical arrangement of lines of authority, communications, rights and duties of an organization. It determines how roles, power and responsibilities are assigned, controlled and coordinated and how information flows between the different levels of management.

Literature also provides materials for the understanding of the concept of organizational chart. In that sense, an organizational chart (often called organization chart, org chart, organigram (me), or organogram) is a diagram that shows the structure of an organization and the relationships and relative ranks of its parts and positions/jobs. This chart is valuable in that it enables one to visualize a complete organization, by means of the picture it presents (Allan Cecil Haskell, Joseph G. Breaznell, 1922).It is defined by the Dictionary-Organizational Behavioral, 2012 as the way a company is set up. Sablynski, 2012 succinctly defined organizational structure as how job tasks are formally divided, grouped, and coordinated. Organizational structure is a set of methods through which, the organization divided into distinct tasks and then create a harmony between different duties (Mintzberg, 1979). Mintzberg original structure types are the Simple Structure, Machine Bureaucracy, Professional Bureaucracy, Divisional Form, and Adhocracy (Mintzberg, 1983). (Underdown, 2012) said organizational structure is the formal system of task and reporting relationships that controls, coordinates, and motivates employees so that they cooperate to achieve an organization's goals. Andrews, 2012 stated that organizational structure "consists of job positions, their relationships to each other and accountabilities for the process and sub-process deliverables". Organizational structure is also defined as the way responsibility and power are allocated, and work procedures are carried out, among organizational members (Ruekert et al, 1985). (Zheng, et al., 2010) mentioned that the most important components of organizational structure include formalization, centralization, and control. Formalization measures the extent to which an organization uses rules and procedures to prescribe behavior. The nature of formalization is the degree to which the workers are provided with rules and procedures that deprive versus encourage creative, autonomous work and learning. In organization with high formalization, there are explicit rules which are likely to impede the spontaneity and flexibility needed for internal innovation (C. J. Chen and J. W. Huang, 2007). Centralization refers to the hierarchical level that has authority to make decision. If decisions are delegated to lower levels the organization is decentralized and if decision making power authority is kept at the top level it is centralized (O. C. Ferrell and S. J. Skinner, 1988). Control in the bureaucracy can consist of rules, standards, and internal procedures (O. C. Ferrell and S. J. Skinner, 1988). Organizational Charts are usually a reactive, rather than a proactive device. It should reflect where you want the organization to go, rather than simply reflects how it is now. According to (Richard Whittington, 2006), organizational structures are concerned with the recurrent relationships between the various members of an organization. This includes not just authority and reporting relationships, the simple question of who is in charge. Organizational structures answer the following questions:

- Who has the resources?
- Who talks to whom?
- Who is accountable for what?
- What can you do on your own?
- What must you do with others?
- What kinds of career paths are available?
- How does knowledge flow around the organization?

Some of these structures are written down formally, in the organizational chart and other procedures. Many of them are informal, even if often closely linked to formal structures as well. Organizational structures are therefore central to achieving anything in an organization. It is an essential part of strategy implementation. It should be proactive and strategic by reflecting a re-envisioned institution that will meet the needs of users now and in the future.

SECTION II: EFFICIENCY

The concept of efficiency, first used in the 1590s, derives from Latin "efficientia" meaning "power to accomplish something," literally referring to efficient power; efficiency; influence. Across literature, it has been defined in various ways. The concept of efficiency expresses a specific form of rationality, used in attempts to control a changing situation by bringing it into conformity with a vision of how the world works (JK Alexande, 2009). In a more general sense, it is the ability to do things well, successfully without waste. It refers to the capacity to produce a specific outcome with a minimum amount of unnecessary effort. Efficiency implies three concepts which are: technical, productive, and allocative. Thus technical efficiency addresses the issue of using given resources to maximum advantage; productive efficiency of choosing different combinations of resources to achieve the maximum benefit for a given cost; and allocative efficiency of achieving the right mixture programmes to maximize benefits (S Palmer - 1999).Efficiency (doing things right) differs from effectiveness (getting things done) in the sense that while the former relates to the ratio of useful output to total input, the latter refers to the ability to achieve a desired result. For example, two companies may achieve the same result but the first one used longer working hours and energy to achieve the desired results while the second

6

used minimum time and efforts to attain the same objectives. In that case the first company is said to be effective while the second will be efficient. This implies that efficiency involves effectiveness in its conception. The following formula illustrated to that effect:

EFFICIENCY= EFFECTIVENESS (Achieving the desired goal) + USEFULNESS (Ratio of useful output to total output)

CHAPTER II: RELATED THEORIES ON ORGANIZATIONAL CHART AND PRESENTATION OF THE CAMEROON CUSTOMS

SECTION I: RELATED THEORIES ON ORGANIZATIONAL CHART

Theories relating to the concept of organizational chart are the same referring to organizational and management theories. Their role is to describe how organization is structured to fulfill their goal and how they interact with the environment. A brief overview of organizational theories will lead us to the bible, Adam Smith, classical theories, neoclassical, institutional theories, systems theories, contingency theories, interactionism, post-modern theories, etc.

i. **PRE-MODERN THEORIES**

- The bible (Exodus 18: 13-23): A recipe is given to us when Moses' father in law recommends him to select worthy men to accompany him in his task as a judge of the nation of Israel running away from Egyptian's captivity;

- Adam Smith (The Wealth of nations, 1776) : The first chapter in An Inquiry into the Nature and Causes of the Wealth of Nations – better known as The Wealth of Nations, published in 1776 – is titled "Of the Division of Labor", and opens with this sentence: "The greatest improvements in the productive powers of labor, and the greater part of the skill, dexterity, and judgment, with which it is anywhere directed, or applied, seem to have been the effects of the division of labor."

- Classical theories:
    - Maw Weber's bureaucracy (protestant ethic and the spirit of capitalism, 1904) : separate areas of competence; written documentation and rules, impersonal interests, expertise and extensive education required for top personnel, clearly defined hierarchy of office, set salaries paid in money;
    - Frederick Winslow Taylor (The principles of scientific management, 1911): "Science, not rule of thumb , Harmony, not discord , Cooperation, not individualism, Maximum output in place of restricted output, The development of each man to his greatest efficiency and prosperity;

- Neoclassical theories:
  - Henri Fayol (1841-1925): French mining engineer and director of mines. Developed a general theory of administration and management. The functions of management are to: Forecast and plan, Organize, Command or direct, Coordinate, Control;
  - Luther Gulick (1892-1993) and Lyndall Urwick (1891-1983), "Papers on the Science of Administration" (1937), founders of Administrative Science Quarterly, strongly influenced by Fayol POSDCORB: What is a manager doing? Planning, organizing, directing, staffing, co-ordinating, reporting, budgeting;
  - Chester Barnard (1886-1961); "The Functions of the Executive", the theories of authority and of incentives. On authority: The channels of communication should be definite; Everyone should know of the channels of communication; Everyone should have access to the formal channels of communication; Lines of communication should be as short and as direct as possible; Competence of persons serving as communication centers should be adequate; The line of communication should not be interrupted when the organization is functioning; Every communication should be authenticated;
  - Herbert A. Simon 1916-2001) –"Administrative Behavior" (1947) – Simon's main interest is in decisions and decision-making. His basic conception is idea of man's bounded rationality – Since the amount information available is always wast and inexhaustable, and we have limited wits, we can never find the best possible solution – The objective "Best way" is therefore not a practical possibility, even if true in theory. Managers will therefore make do with the first solution they find that is deemed good enough. The organization's dependence on the environment is first drawn into the discussion in his cooperation with James March in «Organizations" (1958).

ii.   MODERN THEORIES

- Contingency theories:
    - Joan Woodward (Management and Technology, 1958): Found that organizational form varied, and correlated with production technology and concluded that there was not "one best way" to organize – the nature of the production process would determine which form that would be most suitable;
    - Tom Burns (1913-2001) and G. M. Stalker "The Management of Innovation" (1961) studied the introduction of electronics in Scottish industry. Described two ideal types of organization on each side of a continuum, the mechanistic and the organismic (organic) organization – The organization as a result of the simultaneous working of (at least) three different social systems: • Formal authority: aims, technology, relations with the environment • Cooperative systems of people with different aspirations • The political system – the competition and cooperation for power;
    - Paul R. Lawrence (1922-2011) and Jay W. Lorsch (1932) – "Organization and Environment: Managing Differentiation and Integration" (1967). The organization's effectiveness is judged from the extent to which the members' needs are satisfied through the planned transactions with the environment – In order to cope with the environment, organizations develop units and formal structures suited to the particular environment(s) they operate in;
    - James D. Thompson (1920-1973) – "Organizations in Action" (1967) views organizations as rational, open systems Classifies organizations according to their production technologies and environments : Pooled interdependence (the university), Sequential interdependence (the factory) , Reciprocal interdependence (the airline);
    - Henry Mintzberg –"The Structuring of Organizations" (1979) Synthesized large parts of the organizational research up to ca. 1975. Proposed five basic organizational configurations (forms), each based on

10

one main coordinating mechanism and one key part of the organization: The Simple Structure (Entrepreneurial Form) – based on Direct supervision/ Strategic Apex key, The Machine Bureaucracy based on Standardization of work/ Techno structure key, Professional Bureaucracy based on Standardization of skills, Operating core key, The Adhocracy (Innovative Organization) based on Mutual adjustment, Support staff (R&D) key , The Divisionalized Form (Diversified Organization) based on Standardization of output, Middle line key He later suggested two new configurations: The Missionary Organization based on Standardization of norms, Ideology key and The Political Organization no prime coordinating mechanism, no key part. The structure of an organization can be defined simply as the sum total of the ways in which it divides its labor into distinct tasks and then achieves coordination among them.

- System theories:

    Karl Ludwig von Bertalanffy, Austrian biologist (1901-1972) ; W. Ross Ashby, English psychiatrist (1903-1972); Kenneth Boulding, English/American economist (1910-1993); Anatol Rapaport, Russian/American mathematical psychologist (1911-2007) are the founders of systems theories and according to them: A system: – is composed of parts which must be related (directly or indirectly), else there are really two or more distinct systems is encapsulated (has a boundary) – can be nested inside another system and overlap with other systems, is bounded in time and space, exchanges information and/or material with its environment, consists of processes that transform inputs into output, is dynamic, it evolves, it is self-regulating, i.e. it is self-correcting through feedback, is often composed of entities seeking equilibrium but can exhibit oscillating, chaotic or exponential behavior, can exhibit both multifinality and equifinality.

- Interactionism:
  - David Silverman:"The Theory of Organizations" (1970). Historically, organizational analysis has had a consistent bias toward questions posed by managers. Formal organizations have three main characteristics: They are started at a certain point in time, easy to observe as artefacts .As artefacts; they will be characterized by a patterning of relationships (which is not random). It follows form this that there will be much" attention paid to the discussion and execution of planned changes in social relations, and the 'rules of the game' on which they are based".
  - Karl E. Weick:"The Social Psychology of Organizing" (1969). Enactment: Organizations are enacted; they are created by being talked about. Sense making: Organizations are primarily "sense making systems", incessantly create and recreate conceptions about themselves. Loose coupling: The lack of firmness in the coupling among some of the parts of the organization. Changes can take place locally with little consequence elsewhere.
- Institutional theories:
  - Paul J. DiMaggio and Walter W. Powell, Institutional isomorphism. The question is not why organizations differ, but why there is such an overwhelming degree of homogeneity, why bureaucracy has become the common organizational form. Organizations within the same business may have displayed considerable diversity when first set up, but converge over time toward bureaucracy. They do so not because bureaucracy is the most efficient, but because it furnishes legitimacy in the eyes of outside stakeholders. Three kinds of isomorphism: Coercive isomorphism by political influence, mimetic isomorphism a response to uncertainty , Normative isomorphism as a result of professional managers;
  - John W. Meyer and Brian Rowan: Organization is more about conforming to institutionalized rules than about coordinating and controlling activities. The myth of organizational rationality is necessary

to obtain legitimacy in a society with rationality as the central norm. However, the formal structure comprised of authority structures, plans and rules is only loosely coupled to what is actually done in the organization. Thus, you have two organizational structures, one formal, which can be shaped according to the normative expectations in the environment, and one informal that is actually used for getting things done. The advantages conferred by the myths are stability, legitimacy and resources exactly what is needed to survive.

- Postmodern theories:
  There are two branches of postmodern theory: Epistemological theory (episteme = reason, knowledge): No unequivocal relations between forms of representation (symbols, like words and images) and an objective, external world is possible, we cannot get behind the words. Ontological theory (ontos = being, existence): The society is moving into a new era, which differs from the previous "modern" age in significant ways which can be understood, but not with the old theories. The core of modernity is differentiation in organizations, especially the rational, increasingly fine-grained and rigid division of labor .The core of post modernity is de-differentiation, the gradual integration of jobs, the blurring of areas of responsibility, the increasing overlap of functions, the increasing flexibility, and the team attitudes.

In a nutshell, despite the variety of organizational and management theories, we can realize that they aim at one objective i.e. attaining a specific goal. If at the first place the method designed to that effect was based on rigid and scientific one best way of doing, today it is observed that rationality is subjective, and relative to context (Stewart Clegg, Modern Organizations, 1990). Subjective rationalities can differ widely, as any agent will be heavily influenced by the cultural and institutional values of their national frameworks. Therefore, organizational forms and practices cannot be universal since organizations are human fabrications. They are made out of whatever materials come to hand and can be modified or adopted. Organizations are concocted out of whatever recipe-knowledge is locally available. If an organization is just the product of imitation and copying as most developing countries organizations, it therefore stands great possibilities to fail.

SECTION II: THE ORGANIZATION STRUCTURE OF THE CAMEROON CUSTOMS ADMINISTRATION

The customs administration is defined in its structuring and functioning by Decree N° 2013/066 of 28/02/2013 signed by the Head of State of Cameroon, organizing the Ministry of Finance in the Republic of Cameroon. The missions of the Customs administration are the followings:

• Tax mission: the Customs administration collects taxes and customs duties which are paid into the public treasury. Customs thus contributes to more than 30% in the realization of Cameroon's State budget;

• Economic mission: consists in the protection of the national economic space and the encouragement of the country's economic development. This involves the fight against fraud, smuggling, trade facilitation, management of customs economic regimes, the fight against compensatory measures and dumping, the control of competition rules;

• Assistance mission: Due to its presence at the borders, Customs is required to carry out missions on behalf of other administrations. It thus provides its assistance to various State services, notably: the Ministry of Defense in controlling the entry of weapons, munitions and harmful substances, and the Ministry of Public Health through the control of Drugs and the quality of food;

• Surveillance Mission: the surveillance of land, air, and maritime entry and exit points on the customs territory is provided by the DGC. This surveillance helps to fight against illegal trafficking (drugs, money laundering) and organized crime.

The organization of the Customs administration is structured as follows:
- A Department of Resources and Logistics;
- A Division of International Cooperation and Tax Bases;
- A Division of Legislation and Litigation;
- A Division of Customs Investigations and Surveillance;
- A Division of Recovery, Statistics and Information System;

- A Division for the Control of Financial Operations of External Trade and currency exchange;
- An information and communication Unit;
- Division of Studies, risks management and Trade facilitation;
- A Customs Training Centre;
- A Special Customs Intervention Squad.

The Personnel of the Customs is organized as follows:

Customs staff consists of civil servants and non civil servants. The civil servants include:

• The sedentary personnel, working in principal offices in charge of the determination of the basis of calculation and collection of customs duties and taxes. It is the civilian personnel;

• The active personnel, working in the surveillance units (subdivisions, Brigades, Posts). These personnel fulfills the mission of surveillance of land, sea and air frontiers, the conducting and putting of goods at customs disposal. They wear the uniform of the customs. We find these personnel at central services as well;

• The other civil servants (of the Treasury, Statistics, Water and Forestry, Documentation ...), who perform various functions within the Customs Administration;

• The non-civil servant staff is composed of contract officers of the administration and State agents, all governed by the Labor Code.

i. THE STRUCTURING OF THE CAMEROON CUSTOMS ADMINISTRATION

The customs administration is made up of strategic or central structures, tactical and operational ones as well as particular personnel.

❖ **The strategic or central structures of the customs administration:**

The strategic or central structures of the Cameroon Customs administration are made of 14 units which are presented below. The particularity of these structures or units is that they have a nationwide reach and are in charge of defining the strategy of the administration. They are in other words the central command unit of the Customs, its leadership.

- **The General Manager of Cameroon customs:**

The organizational chart of the Cameroon Customs administration is silent about the details as to the competences required to hold that position. All it says is that he is appointed by the Head of the state and has the rank of a secretary General of a ministry. He is therefore the head and the leader of the Customs administration and as such is in charge of its smooth running, its coordination and the objectives assigned to his administration by the government as stated by Decree N° 2013/066 of 28/02/2013 signed by the Head of State of Cameroon, organizing the Ministry of Finance in the Republic of Cameroon as aforementioned.

- **The Department of Resources and Logistics:**

It is the only unit that has a unit head taking the name of director. This strategic unit is in charge of the provisional and administrative management of the staff; the continuous training of staff; the social policy; the infrastructures and furniture; the budget; the investment policy; acquiring weapon equipment in relation with the ministry of defense; accounting, distribution and mobilization of compensation and benefits; networking and naval equipments management; the follow up of ceremonies such as the march past. It is made up of 03 subunits which are: the human resource and social action subunit, the budget and materials subunit and the transmission and networking subunit.

- **The Division in charge of International Cooperation and Tax Bases:**

Under the authority of a head of unit, it is in charge of international cooperation with sub regional, regional and international related institutions with the Customs administration and questions relating to tariffs and transactional values. It is made up of 02 units: the unit in charge of tariffs and values and the unit in charge of international cooperation.

- **The Division in charge of Legislation and Litigation:**

Under the supervision of a head of unit, the said division is in charge of elaborating customs rules and regulations; the follow up of tariff, value and origin related questions ; follow up of rules and regulations relating to certain specific domains such as oil, mines, agriculture, animal rearing, fishery and copyrights laws; the examination of litigations and claims; the approval of litigation files and distribution of fine and penalties fees; the follow up of law cases as well as the elaboration of data and statistics of customs litigations for the purpose of risk management. It is made up of 03 subunits which are: the customs rules and regulations subunit, the customs regimes subunit and the customs litigations subunit.

16

- **The Division in charge of Customs Investigations and Surveillance:**

Under the authority of a head of unit, it is in charge of posteriori customs controls and the fight against customs fraud, fighting against organized crime, counterfeit and other illegal trafficking as well as the search of information and the control of active services of the Customs administration. It is made up of 04 subunits which are: the investigations brigade in charge of ordinary operations, the investigations brigade in charge of economic operations, the customs monitoring subunit and the unit in charge of following up the planning and implementation of customs controls.

- **The Division in charge of Recovery, Statistics and Information System:**

Under the authority of a head of unit, it is in charge of the customs revenues dashboard; accounting and centralization of customs revenues; follow up of customs revenues; recovery of customs revenues arrears, collecting and producing statistics of external trade; transmission of data to the central bank; taking part in state treasury monthly conference. It is made up of 03 subunits which are: the recovery brigade, the external trade data and statistics analysis unit and customs revenues follow up unit.

- **The Division in charge of the Control of Financial Operations of External Trade and currency Exchange:**

Under the authority of a Head of division having rank of director, The Division in charge of the Control of Financial Operations of External Trade and Exchange is in charge of the enforcement of customs rules and regulations relating to external trade financial and currency transactions, the control of banks and related financial institutions in matters of transfers and currency exchange, the collect, treatment and transfer of statistics of international trade monthly to the central bank, the issue and follow up of not subject import/export declaration, the follow up of export and import bank transfers.

It is made of 02 subunits i.e. the external trade finance control unit and the currency exchange control unit headed by sub directors who have under their authority respectively 04 responsibles for study for the first unit and 03 currency exchange control inspectors plus 06 currency exchange control assistant inspectors for the second unit .

However the organizational chart does not inform us about the requirements to occupy the different posts and duties. It limits itself to the administrative rank assigned to them.

- **The information and communication Unit:**

Placed under the authority of a head of unit, the information and communication unit is in charge of promoting the image of the Customs' administration, implementing communications actions, publishing documentation and rules and regulations of the Customs 'administration , organizing ceremonies of the Customs' administration in collaboration with the department in charge of resources and logistics, animating the website of the Customs and following up relations with the various communications organs. It comprises in addition of his unit head, 04 responsibles in charge of study.

- **Division in charge of Studies, risk management and Trade facilitation:**

Managed by a head of unit, this department is in charge of studies for ameliorating the efficiency of Cameroon Customs' services, elaborating measures for facilitating international trade according to international norms and standards, the follow up of relationship in between the Customs administration and stakeholders as well as the one stop point of international trade, the analysis of the evolution of the economic environment and its impact on customs revenues, the implementation of recommendations for the reform of the customs administration, the production of indicators for the measurement of the control and execution of services, the follow up of performance contracts, the implementation of tools used to enhance efficiency, the extension of performance contracts, animating dialogue in between services and economic operators relating to performance contracts, conception and follow up of management risks, matching data in between NEXUS/EFCOLIA/ASYCUDA, exploitation of fraud notices and litigation data, exploitation of data base of the SGS and the Cameroon Customs administration, proposing criteria for selectivity of some declarations in the red channel in ASYCUDA, the follow up of customs regimes, the analysis of strategic data on certain sensitive products due to their advantageous on the commercial or fiscal point and other analysis assigned the GM. It comprises o3 units: the studies unit, the trade facilitation unit and the risk management unit.

- **The Customs Training Centre:**

It is led by a head of centre and is in charge of elaborating the training planning of the personnel of the Cameroon Customs administration, the implementation of the said training planning, the elaboration of customs teachings programs in collaboration with professional schools and the supervision of trainees. The organizational chart precises that its structuring and functioning will be fixed by a ministerial order.

- **The Special Customs Intervention Squad:**

It is a special unit placed under the authority of a commanding officer and an assistant. This squad is in charge of fighting fraud, smuggling, counterfeiting; the surveillance of waters, air and lands borders in collaboration with the operational units of regional sectors of Customs 'administration, controlling the pentiere, protecting sensitive areas, the management of weapons belonging to the Customs' administration and the follow up of air and sea logistics. It comprises in addition of its managers, the central unit of command and transmission, the information and documentation unit, the maintenance workshop and a customs commissioner. The organizational chart of the Cameroon Customs administration states that the structuring of the subunits listed which are not yet operational will be put in place by a ministerial order.

- **The central litigation fund unit:**

Led by a delegate fund unit head, this unit is in charge of managing the fruits of fines, vacations pay and others. It comprises in addition to the delegate fund unit head, 02 other assistants whose credentials, duties and related requirements are not specified in the organizational chart.

- **The mail delivery and reception unit:**

Placed under the authority of a service head and directly attached to the GM, this service is in charge of: the welcoming of users; the follow up of mails, of individual and collective statutory and regulatory files concerning customs. It is also in charge of the archives. It is made up of 02 subunits. The chart is silent as to the requirements of those in charge of this service.

- **The General manager's Cabinet:**

It is an informal but operational structure of the customs administration. Even though it was not planned by the organizational chart, it is in charge of personal and special tasks and any missions assigned to it by the General Manager of customs. It is led by a chief of cabinet whose competence is only defined superficially by a GM's order and his rank is not determined precisely by any rules and litigations. It is a very important structure in the Customs' administration in the sense that it sometimes plays the role of one or many departments. Its activities are secret and are mastered only by the GM. We can assume that the chief of cabinet also plays the role of technical adviser for any file that is transmitted for appreciation by the GM.

- **The services inspection unit:**

Placed under the authority of a head of inspection, the service inspection is in charge of the audit and internal control of the custom's organization as well as the performance appraisal of the quality of service. It must also guarantee the deontology, the fight against corruption, technical assistance to services. It is also called upon to make proposals for the betterment of the services in their functioning and can also be assigned any other missions by the GM.

Except the head of the structure, it comprises in addition 10 service inspectors all appointed by decree of the prime minister and having rank of assistant director.

- **The IT Division:**

Under the supervision of a head of unit, the IT division is in charge of elaborating and implementing the IT policy of the customs administration, the security and safety of IT equipments, the development and implementation of the NEXUS software, the maintenance of the IT infrastructure and prospective studies regarding the organization of the information system. It comprises 05 subunits which are: IT development subunit, IT security system subunit, NEXUS software management subunit, IT infrastructure technology subunit and networking management subunit.

❖ The tactical structures or units of the customs administration:

Strategy and tactics refer to two separate and distinct organizational functions and practices. Strategy involves planning a company's next move, and tactics involve physically carrying out the plan. The difference between the two concepts can be remembered with the phrase, "strategic is doing the right things -- tactical is doing things right." (Debby Donner, 2016).The tactical units of the Cameroon Customs' administration are: the customs sectors for the civilian corps and the active group command unit.

• The Customs sectors

Under the authority of a chief of sector, the customs sector is in charge of the implementation and follow up of customs rules and regulations in the various regions; the control, coordination, functioning of activities of all customs services at the level of the regions; following up of production and recovery of customs revenues; the management of customs litigations at the regional level; the fight against fraud, smuggling and counterfeit; follow up of imports, exports and currency exchange transactions; management and follow up of human resources. It comprises the following subunits: the communication service, the control brigade, the litigations and auctions sales subunit, the statistic and performance follow up subunits, the administrative affairs subunit, freight management subunit, customs treasury, regional IT center.

The head quarter of customs sectors are located at the siege of the regions except limbe for the south west. The littoral and south regions count each 02 customs sectors. The decree states that other sectors can further be created by order of the minister of finance. The competences of the IT regional center are not clearly specified. Moreover the profiles of those who are supposed to occupy those positions are not identifiable both in the organizational chart and on any other document for that sake.

- **The active group command unit**

Under the authority of a commander in chief, the active group command unit is in charge of the control, coordination, smooth running, supervision, evaluation, follow up and implementation of the action plan of the structures in charge of surveillance. It is made up of an assistant commander, 05 surveillance inspectors and an information research subunit.

❖ **The operational structures or units of the customs administration:**

Strategic plans, tactical plans, and operational plans all work together to move an organization forward and attain its objectives. The difference between them lies in the level of specificity and the level of management which deals with them. Operational structures refer to planning executed by low-level management i.e. when we get to the specific details. As operational structures we can identify the customs houses, the active subdivisions of customs and the operational units of the special intervention group command unit.

- **The Customs houses**

There are 03 types of customs houses which are: the main customs houses, the principal customs houses and the secondary customs houses. The main customs houses are headed by a chief and the said houses is in charge of all possible customs operations in matters of goods clearance. They are made up of subunits such as the customs cash counter, the verification and assessment service, the bonded warehouse service, the temporary admission regime service, the transit management services, the hydrocarbons management services, the central exploitation services and the litigation and benefits management services. The principal customs houses are in charge of specific customs operations and the secondary customs houses are competent for small specific operations. The personnel constituting these houses comprise customs inspectors and attendants of customs.

- **The active subdivisions**

Under the authority of a subdivision head, this unit is in charge of surveillance of the boundaries, ports, airports, train and roads stations in order to search, track fraud, smuggling and counterfeit of goods. They are subdivided into two i.e. commercial and active subdivisions. While the commercial ones are in charge of controlling customs clearing post operations, the active ones are in charge of fight against fraud, smuggling and counterfeit. They have under their supervision, customs brigades and customs posts. If the domains of competences of these various structures are defined, their geographical area of competence is not, as well as the profile and post description relating to them.

- **The other operational units of Customs administration**

The organizational chart of the Customs administration states that other operational units related to the special intervention group command unit are provided which are: the air surveillance subdivision of Douala, the sea surveillance subdivision of kribi, the air and land surveillance control subdivision of Garoua and the transmission and command offices of campo, Mouanko, Idenau, Limbe, Idabato, Moloundou and Kousséri. No other details is given about the organization and functioning of these units.

ii. THE FUNCTIONNING OF THE CAMEROON CUSTOMS ADMINISTRATION

- **Organization of personnel**

The Customs administration comprises 03 categories of personnel: the civil servants of the civilian corps, the civil servants of the paramilitary corps and the personnel who signed a contract with the Customs administration.

The civilian corps is made up of 05 categories which are senior customs inspectors, customs inspectors, customs controllers, assistant customs controllers and customs clerk while for the paramilitary branch, it is constituted of the superior officers, officers, senior warrant officers, warrant officers, brigadier and attendants. The personnel falling under a contract with the customs administration is made up of statisticians, accountants, lawyers, IT specialists, drivers, etc.

- **Analysis of the customs administration's organization**

In this part we shall examine both the strongholds and the limitations of the organizational chart of the Cameroon Customs administration with regards to standards and norms as well as the attainment of its objectives.

In its structuring, the Cameroon Customs administration presents some limitations in its articulation and its visibility as well as its philosophy.

The organizational chart of the Cameroon Customs administration in its structuring, delimitating, and articulating is not harmonious in a way that is pleasant and efficient, in the sense that we can observe several overlapping skills and competences in between the various structures as well as the absence of needed structures thereby creating inertia and conflicts in the organization as presented in the table below.

Table 1: Overlapping skills of the strategic units

N°	Unit 1	Unit 2	Overlapping skills	Observations
1	The services inspection unit	Division of Studies, risks management and Trade facilitation	audit and internal control of the custom's organization as well as the performance appraisal of the quality of service	The 02 units receive files concerning the functioning of customs services and are supposed to provide recommendations.
2	Division of Customs Investigations and Surveillance	A Division for the Control of Financial Operations of External Trade and currency exchange	the control of financial operations in matters of transfers and currency exchange	The 02 units are overlapping regularly in their missions since their skills are not clearly delimitated in that sense
3	Division of Legislation and Litigation	A Division for the Control of Financial Operations of External Trade and currency exchange	The follow up of export repatriation funds	While the organizational chart states that the second unit is in charge of the said following up, the first unit is the one assigned the task on daily ground.
4	IT division	Division of Studies, risks management and Trade facilitation	conception and follow up of management risks	The 02 units are involved in the process and at time it leads to inefficiency and confusion
5	IT division	Department of Resources and Logistics	Networking	While these attributions are those of the second unit, it happens that the technical resources are held

				by the first unit.
6	Division of Recovery, Statistics and Information System	A Division for the Control of Financial Operations of External Trade and currency exchange	Data transfer of external trade to the central bank	The 02 units are given the same attributions by the organizational chart.
7	Special Customs Intervention Squad	Division of Customs Investigations and Surveillance	fight against customs fraud, fighting against organized crime, counterfeit and other illegal trafficking as well as the search of information and the control of active services of the Customs administration	The 02 units share the same competences
8	Division of International Cooperation and Tax Bases	Division of Legislation and Litigation	the follow up of tariff, value and origin related questions	The 02 units share the same competences
9	Customs Training Centre	Department of Resources and Logistics	elaborating the training planning of the personnel of the Cameroon Customs administration, the implementation of the said training planning	The 02 units share the same competences
10	The GM's cabinet	Division of Studies, risks management and Trade facilitation	special tasks and any missions assigned to it by the General	The first unit is informal and playing the role that was supposed to be that of the

				Manager of customs	second unit
11	Central litigation fund unit	Division of Legislation and Litigation	managing the fruits of fines, vacations pay and others	Their collaboration is not sufficiently defined and delimitated
12	Central litigation fund unit	Department of Resources and Logistics	managing the fruits of fines, vacations pay and others	Their collaboration is not sufficiently defined and delimitated
13	information and communication Unit	Department of Resources and Logistics	the follow up of ceremonies such as the march past	Their collaboration is not sufficiently defined and delimitated

Source: The author

PART II: ANALYTICAL FRAMEWORKS: DIAGNOSIS AND RECOMMENDATIONS

CHAPTER III: DIAGNOSIS OF THE SITUATION

SECTION I: DESCRITION OF THE SETTING

The organizational chart of the Cameroon customs department presents limits in its visibility in the sense that there is no official diagram that permits to visualize with ease the various levels of authorities and competences are available.

In its structuring and implementation, no profiles or skills is clearly defined as to who should occupy a specific position therefore leading to any form of subjectiveness that can prove to be inefficient for the organization, and can as well deteriorate the social climate.

In terms of philosophy, the author believes that the organizational chart of the Cameroon Customs administration is not sufficiently proactive in the sense that many units are not yet put in place even though the chart was formalized since 2013.Moreover some of the strategic sub units are still inexistent (no sub directors and agents have been provided formally to the various units for the past 08 months) or not fully operational (many units lack the basic facility such as computers, logistics and other materials to be fully operational) .

I.1. COLLECTION OF DATA

We shall focus on the research design, the target population, the sampling frame, the sample and sampling techniques as well as the research instruments, data collection procedure, the data processing and analysis.

- **Choice of methodology and justification**

In this study, the researcher adopted the concurrent triangulation design that implies converging both quantitative and qualitative data in order to better understand and answer research questions (Martens 2001).

- **Methodology technical characteristics**

Here we shall deal with demographic information, samples and sampling, structures and themes of questionnaires, field work realities and statistical analyses and inferences.

- **Demographic information**

The researcher targeted the personnel of the Cameroon Customs Administration from 2010 to 2016.The figures of the said staff is tabulated below:

Table 2: The personnel of the Cameroon Customs Administration from 2010 to 2016

Year	Total Category A	Total Category B	Total Category C	Total Category D	Total others	Total	Evolution in %
2016							
Men	416	370	685	995	356	2822	53
Wome	118	140	351	548	128	1285	107
2015							
Men	387	350	290	461	360	1848	08.3
Wome	111	132	131	110	135	619	50
2014							
Men	366	333	253	388	366	1706	0.1
Wome n	98	116	34	54	138	440	-01
2013							
Men	366	333	253	376	377	1705	02
Wome	98	116	34	52	144	444	14
2012							
Men	337	315	253	374	389	1668	09
Wome	87	103	34	50	113	387	11

Year	Total Category A	Total Categor y B	Total Category C	Total Categor y D	Total other s	Tota l	Evolutio n in %
2011							
Men	306	287	253	359	314	1519	03
Wome	75	91	34	48	98	346	07
2010							
Men	285	265	253	351	319	1473	
Wome	59	81	34	44	104	322	

Source: Service of personnel of the Cameroon Customs Administration.

- **Samples and sampling**

Sample is defined as a part of a large population (Orodho and KIM, 2009), which is thought to be representative of the larger population. This is the reason why the above-mentioned sampling frame was chosen.

The sample for the study is comprised of 275 employees draw from the 3895 personnel constituting the Cameroon Customs administration. A total of 260 questionnaires were distributed to selected employees. Out of these, 250 questionnaires were duly filled and returned.10 questionnaires distributed were not returned. We assert the response rate to 88, 5 % around.

- **Structures and themes of the questionnaires**

Questionnaires with both open ended and closed questions were used to establish the relationship in between organization of the Cameroon Customs administration and its performance in the domains of career advancement; work life balance practices; motivation and retention of personnel.

- **Field's Work realities**

Field research or fieldwork is the collection of information outside a laboratory, library or workplace setting. The author could not work in quiet and orderly place since managers dealt with the same issues several times, for short periods of time in a strong complexity and lack of data (Aktouf (2006, p. 198).

- **Statistical analyses and inferences**

The study sought furthermore to establish the perceived relationship between organizational chart, and organizational performance. In the Analysis of variance setting, the observed variance in a Particular variable is partitioned into components attributable to different sources of variation. ANOVA provides a statistical test of whether or not the means of several groups are equal, and therefore generalizes the t-test to more than two groups.

Organizational chart was found significant to organizational performance ($r = .219$, $p = .000$) and workforce planning was significantly related to organizational performance ($r = .167$, $p = .003$).

Table 3: Correlations between organizational chart, Workforce planning and organizational performance

Independent variables	Pearson correlation	Organizational performance
Organizational chart	Sig. (1-tailed) N	219 .000 259
Workforce planning	Sig. (1-tailed) N	167 .003 260

Source: The author

---

7. Aktouf (2006, p. 198) summed-up Mintzberg observations about what takes place in the field: 'First, the manager's job is not ord.

- **Research Variables**

Figure 1: Illustration of the Research variables

Independent variable   dependent variable

Organizational chart   ————————————————→ organizational performance

- **Research hypotheses**

A research hypothesis can be as a specific, clear, and testable proposition or predictive statement about the possible outcome of a scientific research (Good & Hatt). In other words it is a tentative answer to a research problem that is advanced. It describes in concrete terms what you expect will happen in your study. The hypotheses created when speculating upon the outcome of our research or experiment are the followings:

> H_O: organizational chart does not influence organizational performance
> H_1: organizational chart influences organizational performance

- **Limitations of the research methodology**

Although this research was carefully prepared, I am still aware of its limitations and shortcomings. First of all, the research was conducted in the developing world context where access to information is still very limited. Secondly, the population of the experimental group does not systematically represent the majority of workers. Thirdly, the research in this area is scarce in Africa in general and in Cameroon in particular, the country of the researcher. Finally since the assessment of the pretest and post test was conducted by the author himself, it is possible to find in this study a certain degree of subjectivity.

SECTION II: ANALYSIS AND INTERPRETATION OF DATA

In this part we shall present in one hand the results of our statistical analyses based on our hypotheses, research variables, literature and theoretical review as well as methodology. On the other hand we shall carry out the discussion of our study.

- **Analysis results and interpretations**

In order to describe and explore the link in between organizational performance and organizational chart. Data of the Cameroon Customs administration were collected and furthermore analyzed.

The above tables show the demographic information related to the personnel of the Customs administration. We can observe that for the year 2016, we registered 416 men for 118 women. In 2015, 387 men for 111 women. In 2014, 366 men for 98 women, the same figures in 2013. In 2012, 337 men for 87 women. In 2011 306 men for 75 women. And in 2010, 285 men for 59 women.

The researcher focused his studies on the most recent data i.e. 2017 as represented by the table 9 below:

Table 4: The civil branch of the Customs Administration.

Grades	Men	Women	Total
Senior customs inspectors	67	5	72
Inspectors	120	48	168
Senior customs controllers	36	10	46
Controllers	88	40	128
Assistant controllers	212	117	329
Agents	216	183	399
Total	**739**	**403**	**1142**

Source: The HRM Department of the Customs Administration

For the achievement of the objectives of this study, research hypotheses were formulated and tested based on the literature review on HRM practices and structure organization as well as organizational performance. The statistical test results (regression and correlation analyses) of each null hypothesis at 94 % confidence level.

Table 5: Interviews

	Frequency	Percentages
Strongly Agree	45	25
Agree	90	50
Neutral	9	5
Disagree	18	10
Strongly Disagree	18	10
Total	180	100

Source: Author

The table shows that 90% of the participants indicated that organization structuring can lead to organizational performance.

The outcomes of this research work have clearly revealed that all independent variable (organizational chart) has a direct and positive correlation and influence over the dependent variable (Organizational performance).

This has been done through the following process: Demographic information; Response rate; examination of Research Hypotheses; Collective role of the independent variables on the dependent variable and Analysis based on research objectives. Those analysis were based on a correlation and statistics inferences in between the independent variables themselves and after by perusing the link in between the independent variable and the dependent one.

- **Discussion**

The objective of our study was to interpret and describe the significance of organizational chart on the organizational performance, focusing on the case study of the Cameroon Customs administration. Comparing with the above mentioned literature review and theoretical frameworks; it appears that the advantages of the above mentioned independent variables (organizational chart) are as follows: helps build and design the organization structure to meet the business' objectives; guide the employees to know their rights and responsibilities; help divide the functions of a company, enterprise or department; shows the relationships between the organization's staff members; With organizational chart, it's easy to find whether the officer's workload is too heavy; it is easy to find whether the unrelated persons undertake the work of several loose, no relationship; find out whether an employee is incompetent in this work at important positions; make everyone clear within their organizations and improve employee performance; other departments are also able to understand and enhance the coordination of the organization; it's easy to see the promotion channels open; some managers can use the organizational chart tool to analyze budget, design work team and generate reports and outline employee tasks and which manager is responsible for overseeing each employee (Edraw, 2018).This is in line with authors cited above and the theories presented.

This means that organization structure as well as organizational chart have a significant impact on organizational performance as regards to the hypothesis formulated and to the research .However the literature review and theories above stated show limits in the sense that public service is characterized as far as mobility is concerned with socio-political realities such as regional balance and sociological representativeness that play an important role in the peace and stability of a country. The said literature did not also provide enough tools to resolve issues relating to the impact in between our two variables. Moreover the questions concerning the contextualization and the implementation of the general interest and performance are insufficiently provided by the surveyed literature and theoretical frameworks.

Henceforth it appears glaringly clear that there is a need to restructure the organization structure of the Customs department with regard to the insufficiency of clear lines of communication and the existing overwhelming overlapping competences and skills in order to develop organizational performance in African institutions such as the Cameroon Customs Administration considering its own social realities, objectives and historical background.

CHAPTER IV: ENHANCING EFFICIENCY IN THE CAMEROON CUSTOMS

SECTION I: RECOMMENDATIONS ANALYSIS

From the above mentioned, the following recommendations are formulated towards the Cameroon Customs management:

1) **Restructuring the organizational chart of the strategic units of the Cameroon Customs administration as illustrated below:**

   - Reshaping the department of resources and logistics into two different units which will be the director of Human resource and the director of supply and real estates ; the director of human resource will absorb the competences of the customs training center;

   - The 02 departments of customs investigations and surveillance plus that of finance, external trade and currency exchange should form a unique department in charge of customs investigations considering their numerous overlapping skills and conflicts;

   - A director of surveillance will be created that will exercise all functions hitherto assumed by both the division of customs investigations and surveillance as well as the special customs intervention squad;

   - The services inspector becomes the director of audit and internal control to avoid overlapping skills with the director of studies, trade facilitation and risks analysis;

   - The director of studies, trade facilitation and international cooperation is a fusion of the division of studies, trade facilitation and risks analysis stripped from the last competence with the attributions of the division of international cooperation and tax bases. This is justified by the fact that studies, trade facilitation and international cooperation are strongly stringed, while risk management most often goes with IT in our Cameroonian context as will be illustrated later;

   - The Director of legal affairs and litigations keep the same functions but the management of any monetary transactions formerly exercised by them is transferred to the director of human resource for centralization, efficiency and equity necessary for the motivation of the human resource of the organization;

- The Director of recovery and statistics keep the same functions but with an internal restructuration, moreover this unit is accordingly the unique one in charge of transmission of data to the central bank;
- The Director of IT, networking and risks management will be transferred networking and risks management respectively from the director of human resource and the one in charge of studies because of the strong ties in between these attributions and for efficiency purposes.
- The Sub director of mails management and translation as well as the one in charge of communication, information and public relations keep essentially the same functions with the difference that the first one has seen added competence on translation due to serious shortages noticed in that domain. The second one has seen added the public relations aspect to better the promotion of the image of the Customs administration

> **The Director of Human Resource (DRH):** He is in charge of Planning of human resource, organizing HR, directing HR, controlling HR, recruitment, hiring, job analysis and design, performance appraisal, training and development, compensation and benefits, employee welfare, labor relations, personnel records and personal research.
>
> The department of HR will comprise the following sub directors assisted by the head of services referred into brackets: The sub director of recruitment, training and career management (service of recruitment and training; service of career management), the sub director of organization and employee welfare (service of organization and studies; service of social welfare), the sub director of performance appraisal and remunerations (service of performance appraisal and service of remunerations).
>
> The service of recruitment and training will be in charge of : Identify Vacancy and Evaluate Need ;Develop Position Description ;Develop Recruitment Plan; Select Search Committee; Post Position and Implement Recruitment Plan; Review Applicants and Develop Short List; Conduct Interviews; Assess Organizational Training & Development Needs ; Define Training Objectives; Training Program Design; Adopt Training Principles for agents; Training Program

Development; Training Program Implementation; Evaluate Your Training Program. The head of service must have received a specialized training in HR; economics; laws or social sciences. He will be assisted in his functions by 01 statistician, 01 IT expert and 03 HR specialists.

The service of career management will be in charge of planning, supervising, controlling, handling, coping and administrating the professional life of Customs agents. The service will comprise 05 agents in addition to the head of service. The head of service must have received a specialized training in HR; economics; laws or social sciences. He will be assisted in his functions by 01 statistician, 01 IT expert and 03 HR specialists.

The service of organization and studies will be in charge of the management of the information system of HR; centralize statistics of the HR department, analysis on the organizational chart; studies on HR. The service will comprise 05 agents in addition to the head of service. The head of service must have received a specialized training in HR; economics; laws or social sciences. He will be assisted in his functions by 01 statistician, 01 IT expert and 03 HR specialists.

The service of employees welfare will be in charge of the safety and wellbeing of employees i.e. provision of loans, medical facilities, retirement benefits, education facilities for the employee's and their families, housing benefits, sporting facilities, funeral facilities, etc. The service will comprise 05 agents in addition to the head of service The head of service must have received a specialized training in HR; economics; laws or social sciences. He will be assisted in his functions by 01 statistician, 01 IT expert and 03 HR specialists.

The service of performance appraisal will be in charge of Establish Performance Standards; Communicating Performance Expectations to Employees; Measure Actual Performance; Compare Actual Performance with Standards; Discuss the Appraisal with the Employee and Initiate Corrective Action. The service will comprise 05 agents in addition to the head of service. The head of service must have received a specialized training in HR; economics; laws or social sciences. He will be assisted in his functions by 01 statistician, 01 IT expert and 03 HR specialists.

The service of remunerations will be in charge of setting an equitable compensatory system; develop motivating salary ranges; compensation and benefits audits; defining benefit packages; to ensure harmony in between compensation and benefits with performance management system; put in place a comprehensive compensation strategy and compliance with legal requirements. The service will comprise 05 agents in addition to the head of service. The head of service must have received a specialized training in HR; economics; laws or social sciences. He will be assisted in his functions by 01 statistician, 01 IT expert and 03 HR specialists.

> **The director of supply and real estates (DAP):** He is in charge of Handling financial operations of the property; Prepare and maintain financial statements; Negotiate contracts for janitorial, security, landscaping, trash removal, and other services; Monitor the performance of contractors; Investigate and resolve complaints from units when services are not properly provided; Purchase supplies and equipment for properties; Hire contractors to make repairs; Supervise maintenance; the budgeting ; the investment policy ; accounting .

The department of supply and real estates will comprise the following sub directors assisted by the head of services referred into brackets: The sub director of budget, logistics and transports (the service of budget and finance; the service of logistics and transports); the sub director of real estate property (the service of facility management, the service of risk management and compliance).

The service of budgeting is in charge of setting financial needs for the running of the organization; determining current and updated financial situations; incomes controlling; expenditures tracking; categorizing expenditures; creating budget spreadsheet and information system; balancing budget and following up budget discipline and managing payments ordered exclusively by the GM. The said payments which must be made through the bank account of the Cameroon customs administration will be done through bank transfers and exceptionally in cash by order of the GM after duly valid justifications. The service will comprise 05 agents in addition to the head of service. The head of service must have received a specialized training in accounting or related sciences. He will be assisted in his functions by 01 statistician, O1 IT expert and 03 budgeting specialists.

The service of logistics and transports will be in charge of materials handling, production, packaging, inventory, transportation, warehousing, and security of physical items; acquiring and managing transportation means of personnel and goods thatincludes automobiles, bicycles, buses, trains, trucks, helicopters, watercraft, spac ecraft and aircraft, etc. The service will comprise 05 agents in addition to the head of service. The head of service must have received a specialized training in logistics and transports or related sciences. He will be assisted in his functions by 01 statistician, O1 IT expert and 03 logistics and transportation specialists.

The service of facility management will be in charge of managing housing facilities for customs administration and personnel; maintenance of buildings and equipments; renovations; property management agreement; land insurances and taxes. The service will comprise 05 agents in addition to the head of service. The head of service must have received a specialized training in real estate property management or related sciences. He will be assisted in his functions by 01 building engineer; 01 laws specialist and 03 real estate property maintenance technicians.

The service of risk management and compliance control will be in charge of conducting audits and internal controls on building ; routine inspections; building reports; follow up public contracts procedures ; employing static or dynamic hedges to reduce risks; studies and statistics. The service will comprise 05 agents in addition to the head of service. The head of service must have received a specialized training in real estate property management or related sciences. He will be assisted in his functions by 01 building engineer; 01 laws specialist and 03 real estate property specialists.

➢ The director of Customs investigations (DED): He is in charge of the Control of posteriori customs controls; Financial Operations of External Trade and Exchange ; the enforcement of customs rules and regulations relating to external trade financial and currency transactions, the control of banks and related financial institutions in matters of transfers and currency exchange, the collect, treatment and transfer of statistics of international trade monthly to the division in charge of statistics , the issuing and following up of not subject import/export declaration, the following up of export and import bank transfers.

The department of customs investigations will comprise the following sub directors assisted by the head of services referred into brackets: The sub director of Customs commercial transactions (the service of ordinary operations regimes, the service of special regimes); the sub director of finance, trade and currency exchange operations (the service of finance and external trade operations, the service of currency exchange operations)

The service of ordinary operations regime will be in charge of the planning, controlling, and assessment of posteriori customs controls relating to ordinary regimes. The service will comprise 05 agents in addition to the head of service. The head of service must have received a specialized training or a large experience of at least 05 years in customs investigations procedures and techniques. He will be assisted in his functions by 01 statistician; 01 laws specialist and 03 customs officers.

The service of special operations regimes will be in charge of the planning, controlling, and assessment of posteriori customs controls relating to special customs regimes. The service will comprise 05 agents in addition to the head of service. The head of service must have received a specialized training or a large experience of at least 05 years in customs investigations procedures and techniques. He will be assisted in his functions by 01 statistician; 01 laws specialist and 03 customs officers.

The service of finance and trade operations will be in charge of the enforcement of customs rules and regulations relating to external trade financial and currency transactions, the control of banks and related financial institutions in matters of transfers and currency exchange, the collect, treatment and transfer of statistics of international trade monthly to the division in charge of statistics , the issuing and following up of not subject import/export declaration, the following up of export and import bank transfers. The service will comprise 05 agents in addition to the head of service. The head of service must have received a specialized training or a large experience of at least 05 years in customs investigations procedures and techniques.

He will be assisted in his functions by 01 statistician; 01 laws specialist, 01 banking and finance specialist and 02 customs officers.

The service of currency exchange will be in charge of implementing the laws and regulations in matters of currency exchange; related statistics; fighting against money laundering; planning, controlling, directing and evaluating the strategy for effective repatriation of funds in collaboration with the active units who must report to him monthly. The service will comprise 05 agents in addition to the head of service. The head of service must have received a specialized training or a large experience of at least 05 years in customs investigations procedures and techniques. He will be assisted in his functions by 01 statistician; 01 laws specialist, 01 banking and finance specialist and 02 customs officers.

➤ The Director of Customs surveillance (DSD): He is in charge of Reporting, data accumulation, collecting the data, data analysis, fighting against fraud , smuggling, counterfeiting; the surveillance of waters, air and lands borders in collaboration with the operational units of regional sectors of Customs administration, controlling the pentiere, protecting sensitive areas, the management of weapons belonging to the Customs' administration and the follow up of air, land and sea logistics relating to the surveillance system, the follow up of paramilitary activities and coordination of march past by customs agents.

The department of customs surveillance will comprise the following sub directors assisted by the head of services referred into brackets: The sub director of customs intelligence and programming (the service of customs intelligence, the service of analysis and programming); the sub director of customs special interventions (the service of the fight against fraud, the service of equipment and paramilitary operations).

The service of customs intelligence will be in charge of reporting, statistics, data accumulation, collecting the data, data analysis necessary for the implementation of the surveillance strategy of the customs administration. The service will comprise 05 agents in addition to the head of service. The head of service must have received a specialized training or a large experience of at least 05 years in customs investigations procedures, economic intelligence and techniques. He will be assisted in his functions by 01 statistician; 01 laws specialist, 01 economics and finance specialist and 02 customs officers.

The service of analysis and programming will be in charge of planning, controlling, directing and evaluating the surveillance strategy and the fight against customs fraud and related economic crimes. The service will comprise 05 agents in addition to the head of service. The head of service must have received a specialized training or a large experience of at least 05 years in customs investigations procedures, economic intelligence and techniques. He will be assisted in his functions by 01 statistician, 01 IT specialist, 01 laws specialist, 01 economics and finance specialist and 01 customs officers.

The service of the fight against fraud will be in charge of the operational fight against fraud, smuggling, counterfeiting, the surveillance of waters, air and lands borders in collaboration with the operational units of regional sectors of Customs administration, controlling the pentiere, protecting sensitive areas. The service will comprise 50 agents in addition to the head of service. The head of service must have received a specialized training or a qualified experience of 05 years minimum in military surveillance techniques. He will be assisted in his functions by 10 customs officers and 40 customs agents of lower ranks.

The service of equipment and paramilitary operations will be in charge of the management of weapons belonging to the Customs administration and the follow up of air, land and sea logistics relating to the surveillance system, the follow up of paramilitary activities and coordination of march past by customs agents. The head of service must have received a specialized training or a qualified experience of 05 years minimum in military surveillance techniques. He will be assisted in his functions by 10 customs officers and 40 customs agents of lower ranks.

➤ The Director of audit and internal control(DCI): He will be in charge of the audit and internal control of the custom's administration as well as the performance appraisal of the quality of service, the respect of legal procedures by the various services, the examination of the effectiveness of the organizational system through respect of separation of duties, time management, decorum, checks and balances, safeguarding of records, the training level and competence of employees, etc. It is also in charge of guaranteeing the deontology, the fight against corruption and provides technical assistance to services when required. It is also called upon to make proposals for the betterment of the services in their functioning and can also be assigned any other missions by the GM.

The department of audit and internal control will comprise the following sub directors assisted by the services referred to in brackets: The sub director of strategic and tactical units (the service of strategic units, the service of tactical units) and the sub director of operational units (the service of sedentary units, the service of active units).

The service of strategic units (directorates and assimilated units of the headquarter of customs administration) will be in charge of the audit and internal control of the strategic units as well as the performance appraisal of the quality of service of these units. The service will comprise a head of service who must be a senior auditor by training, specialization or at least 10 years in the domain. He will be assisted in his functions by 01 statistician and junior auditors who must have received specialized training or at least 05 years experience in auditing and internal control. It should be provided as much as junior auditors corresponding to the numbers of strategic units in reason of at least one junior auditor in charge of a specific unit.

The service of tactical units (sectors and active group command units) will be in charge of the audit and internal control of the tactical units as well as the performance appraisal of the quality of service of these units. The service will comprise a head of service who must be a senior auditor by training, specialization or at least 10 years in the domain. He will be assisted in his functions by 01 statistician and junior auditors who must have received specialized training or at least 05 years experience in auditing and internal control. It should be provided as much as junior auditors corresponding to the numbers of tactical units in reason of at least one junior auditor in charge of a specific unit.

The service of sedentary units (customs houses) will be in charge of the audit and internal control of the tactical units as well as the performance appraisal of the quality of service of these units. The service will comprise a head of service who must be a senior auditor by training, specialization or at least 10 years in the domain. He will be assisted in his functions by 01 statistician and 10 junior auditors who must have received specialized training or at least 05 years experience in auditing and internal control.

The service of operational units (active subdivisions) will be in charge of the audit and internal control of the tactical units as well as the performance appraisal of the quality of service of these units. The service will comprise a head of service who must be a senior auditor by training, specialization or at least 10 years in the domain. He will be assisted in his functions by 01 statistician and 10 junior auditors who must have received specialized training or at least 05 years experience in auditing and internal control.

> The Director of studies, trade facilitation and international cooperation (DEF): He is in charge of making propositions and carry out studies to clarify the GM on certain matters of customs affairs, participate in the preparation of the finance laws, analyzing the evolution of economic, financial and social events, following up the evolution of the international environment, participate in the evaluation of impact studies of international environment on customs administration, participate in the evaluation of sectorial policies, putting in place tools for data analysis in the customs administration as well as the development of data necessary for attaining customs objectives, elaborating and evaluating measures for facilitating international trade according to international norms and standards, the follow up of relationship in between the Customs administration and stakeholders as well as the one stop point of international trade, the analysis of the evolution of the economic environment and its impact on customs revenues, the implementation of recommendations for the reform of the customs administration, following up cooperation with all international stakeholders and partners, studies on questions of transactional values, origin, tariffs and related questions.

The directorate of studies, trade facilitation and international cooperation will comprise 03 sub directors who will be assisted by 06 heads of services as follows:

The sub director of studies (the service of national environment analyses and prospective, the head of service of international environment analyses and prospective); The sub director of trade facilitation (the service of norms and standards, the service of relationships with national stakeholders) ; The sub director of international cooperation (the service of international relations, the service of tax bases).

The service of national environment analyses and prospective will be in charge of making propositions and carry out studies to clarify the GM on certain matters of national customs affairs, participate in the preparation of the finance laws, carrying out prospective studies on the evolution of the national environment's impact on customs performances, analyzing the evolution of national economic, financial and social events , participate in the evaluation of sectorial policies, putting in place tools for data analysis in the customs administration as well as the development of data necessary for attaining customs objectives. The service will comprise a head of service who must be a researcher of high profile in social sciences, he will be assisted by 03 research assistant officers specialized in research studies or having qualified experience of at least 10 years in the customs administration and 01 expert in prospective sciences.

The service of international environment analyses and prospective will be in charge of making propositions and carry out studies to clarify the GM on certain matters of international customs affairs, collaborate in the preparation of the finance laws, carrying out prospective studies on the evolution of the international environment's impact on customs performances, analyzing the evolution of international economic, financial and social events, participate in the evaluation of impact studies of international environment on customs administration, collaborate in the evaluation of sectorial policies, collaborate in putting in place tools for data analysis in the customs administration as well as the development of data necessary for attaining customs objectives. The service will comprise a head of service who must be a researcher of high profile in social sciences, he will be assisted by 03 research assistant officers specialized in research studies or having qualified experience of at least 10 years in the customs administration and 01 expert in prospective sciences.

The service of norms and standards will be in charge of seeking information about appropriate norms and standards, seeking information about accreditation and certification processes, participate in norms and standards workshops, follow up respect of international norms and standards in customs procedures, organize training in questions of norms, standards and certification, participate in evaluation of policies in matters of norms and standards, follow up relationships with technical stakeholders in matters of norms and standards, carry out studies on norms and standards impacting on customs revenues. The service will comprise a head of service who must be an expert in norms, standards and certification procedures, he will be assisted by 03 research assistant officers specialized in international norms and standards or having qualified experience of at least 10 years in the customs administration and 01 expert in prospective sciences.

The service of relationships with national stakeholders will be in charge of the follow up of relationship in between the Customs administration and stakeholders as well as the one stop point of international trade, the organization of workshops, seminars, forum or any ceremony with the national stakeholders, the follow of resolutions or meetings with stakeholders, the treatment of their observations and their performance, making proposals for resolution of eventual conflicts in between stakeholders and the customs administration. The service will comprise a head of service that must have an experience of at least 10 years in the customs administration; he will be assisted by 03 research assistant officers having qualified experience of at least 05 years in the customs administration and 01 expert in prospective sciences.

The service of international relations will be in charge of following up cooperation with all international stakeholders and partners such as the World Customs Organization, IMF, World Bank, CEMAC, and CEEAC, etc. They will be in charge of following all activities and projects with such institutions, related data analysis, statistics and proposal for efficient collaboration. The service will comprise a head of service that must be an expert in international relations or related sciences; he will be assisted by 03 research assistant officers having qualified experience of at least 05 years in the customs administration and 01 expert in project management.

The service of tax bases will be in charge of studies on questions of transactional values, origin, tariffs and related questions, the production and evaluation of data bases on transactional values, origin, tariffs and related questions, the treatment, analysis of any specific questions or litigations on such aspects. The service will comprise a head of service that must be an expert in tax bases or having a qualified experience of at least 15 years in the customs administration; he will be assisted by 03 research assistant officers having qualified experience of at least 10 years in the customs administration and 01 statistician.

➢ The Director of legal affairs and litigations (DAJ): He will be in charge of elaborating and analyzing every issues relating to customs rules and regulations; follow up of rules and regulations relating to certain specific domains such as oil, mines, agriculture, animal rearing, fishery and copyrights laws, etc; the examination of litigations and claims; the approval of litigation files; the follow up of law cases as well as the elaboration of data and statistics of customs litigations.

It will comprise in addition of the director, 02 sub directors assisted by 04 head of services as follows: The sub director of legislation (the service of national laws, the service of international laws), the sub director of litigations (the service of lawsuits, the service of customs litigations files).

The service of national laws will be in charge of elaborating and analyzing every issues relating to customs rules and regulations at the national level; follow up of rules and regulations relating to certain specific domains at the national level such as oil, mines, agriculture, animal rearing, fishery and copyrights laws. In addition to the head of the structure who must be an expert in laws issues, it will comprise 05 research officers who must be specialized in laws issues.

The service of international laws will be in charge of elaborating and analyzing every issues relating to customs rules and regulations at the international level; follow up of rules and regulations relating to certain specific domains at the international level such as oil, mines, agriculture, animal rearing, fishery and copyrights laws. In addition to the head of the structure who must be an expert in laws issues, it will comprise 05 research officers who must be specialized in laws issues.

The service of lawsuits will be in charge of following up law disputes involving the customs administration; they will have as responsibility initial Pleadings, disclosures, discovery, motions, trial, post-Trial Motions and Appeals, etc. They will also be in charge of following up of swearing oath ceremonies and related issues. In addition to the head of the structure who must be an expert in laws issues, it will comprise 05 research officers who must be specialized in laws issues.

The service of customs litigations files will be in charge of the examination of litigations and claims; the approval of litigation files; the follow up of law cases as well as the elaboration of data and statistics of customs litigations. In addition to the head of the structure who must be an expert in laws issues or having an experience of at least 05 years experience in the customs administration , it will comprise 05 research officers who must customs agents by profession.

➢ The Director of Recovery and Statistics (DSR): He will be in charge of the customs revenues dashboard; accounting and centralization of customs revenues; follow up of customs revenues; recovery of customs revenues arrears, collecting and producing statistics of external trade; transmission of data to the central bank; taking part in state treasury monthly conference.

It will comprise in addition of the director, 02 sub directors assisted by 04 heads of services as follows: The sub director of customs revenues control (the service of follow up of customs revenues, the service of arrears recovery), the sub director of statistics (the service of data analysis, the service of performance).

The service of customs revenues follow up will be in charge of the customs revenues dashboard; accounting and centralization of customs revenues; follow up of customs revenues. In addition to the head of the structure who must be an expert in statistics, it will comprise 03 research officers who must be specialized in statistics or related sciences.

The service of arrears recovery will be in charge of the recovery of customs revenues arrears. In addition to the head of the structure who must be an expert in statistics, it will comprise 10 senior customs research officers and 20 junior customs research officers who must be specialized in statistics, accounting, economics or related sciences.

The service of data analysis will be in charge of the collecting and producing of statistics of external trade; centralization and transmission of data to the central bank. In addition to the head of the structure who must be an expert in statistics, banking, economics or related sciences, it will comprise 04 customs research officers who must be specialized in statistics, accounting, economics or related sciences.

The service of performance will be in charge of conceiving; following up and evaluation of customs performance tools for the various customs units, and it will be in charge to make studies for assigning realistic customs revenues objectives for each unit of the customs administration. In addition to the head of the structure who must be an expert in statistics, banking, economics or related sciences, it will comprise 05 customs research officers who must be specialized in statistics, accounting, economics or related sciences.

➤ The Director of IT, networking and risk management (DIR): He will be in charge of is in charge of elaborating and implementing the IT policy of the customs administration, the security and safety of IT equipments, the development and implementation of the NEXUS software, the maintenance of the IT infrastructure and prospective studies regarding the organization of the information system , conception and follow up of management risks, matching data in between NEXUS/EFCOLIA/ASYCUDA, exploitation of fraud notices and litigation data, exploitation of data base of the SGS and the Cameroon Customs administration, proposing criteria for selectivity of some declarations in the red channel in ASYCUDA, the follow up of customs regimes in the computer system , the analysis of strategic data on certain sensitive products due to their advantageous on the commercial or fiscal point and other analysis assigned the GM, networking, transmissions and telecommunications.

It will comprise in addition of the director, 02 sub directors assisted by 06 heads of services as follows: The sub director of IT (the service of maintenance, the service of security, the service of networking and transmissions), the sub director of data treatment and risks management (the service of data treatment, the service of risks management).

The service of maintenance will be in charge of elaborating and implementing the IT policy of the customs administration, the development and implementation of the NEXUS software, the maintenance of the IT infrastructure and prospective studies regarding the organization of the information system. In addition to the head of the structure who must be an IT engineer specialized in maintenance, it will comprise 03 assistants IT specialist in maintenance and 03 specialists in IT development.

The service of security will be in charge of the security and safety of IT equipments. In addition to the head of the structure who must be an IT engineer specialized in security systems, it will comprise 05 assistants IT specialist in security systems.

The service of networking and transmissions will be in charge of questions relating to the development, management of networking, transmissions and telecommunications. In addition to the head of the structure who must be a telecoms engineer, it will comprise 05 assistants telecoms specialists.

The service of data treatment will be in charge of collecting, analyzing data in the systems, create relevant data bases on external trade, and treat demands in terms of data analysis in the computer systems of the customs administration, matching data in between NEXUS/EFCOLIA/ASYCUDA, exploitation of data base of the SGS and the Cameroon Customs administration. In addition to the head of the structure who must be a customs agent having acquired a significant experience of at least 05 years, it will comprise 02 customs assistant research officers and 03 statisticians.

The service of risks management will be in charge of conception and follow up of management risks, exploitation of fraud notices and litigation data, proposing criteria for selectivity of some declarations in the red channel in ASYCUDA, the follow up of customs regimes in the computer system, the analysis of strategic data on certain sensitive products due to their advantageous on the commercial or fiscal point and other analysis assigned the GM. In addition to the head of the structure who must be a customs agent having acquired a significant experience of at least 05 years, it will comprise 02 customs assistant research officers and 03 statisticians.

➢ The sub director of mails management and translation (SDC): He will be in charge of the welcoming of users; the follow up of mails, following up of individual and collective statutory and regulatory files concerning customs, the management of the archives, the conception and implementation of the mails automation, translation of official documents in collaboration with the unit in charge at the ministry of finance.

It will comprise in addition of the sub director, 02 services as follows: the mails management service and the service of translation.

The service of mails management will be in charge of the welcoming of users; the follow up of mails, following up of individual and collective statutory and regulatory files concerning customs, the management of the archives, the conception and implementation of the mails automation. In addition to the head of service who must be specialized in archiving, it will also comprise 02 assistants equally specialized in archiving, 01 customs research officer and 01 statistician.

The service of translation will be in charge of translation of official documents in collaboration with the unit in charge at the ministry of finance. In addition to the head of service who must be specialized in translation and interpretation, it will also comprise 02 assistants specialized in translation, 01 customs research officer and 01 IT expert.

➢ The Sub director of communication, information and public relations (SDI): He will be in charge of the information and communication unit is in charge of promoting the image of the Customs' administration, implementing communications actions, publishing documentation and rules and regulations of the Customs 'administration , organizing ceremonies of the Customs' administration in collaboration with the department in charge of resources and logistics, animating the website of the Customs and following up relations with the various communications organs.

It will comprise in addition of the sub director, 02 services as follows: the communication service and the information and public relations service.

The communication service will be in charge of publishing documentation as well as rules and regulations of the Customs 'administration, organizing ceremonies of the Customs' administration, animating the website of the Customs department. In addition to the head of service who must be specialized in communication, it will also comprise 02 assistants equally specialized in communication , 01 customs research officer and 01 IT expert specialized in web mastering.

The information and public relations service will be in charge of developing public relations strategies and campaigns, preparing press releases, keynote speeches and promotional material. Building positive relationships with stakeholders, media and the public. In addition to the head of service who must be specialized in information and public relations techniques , it will also comprise 02 assistants equally specialized in the same fields , 01 customs research officer and 01 IT expert specialized in web mastering.

2) Restructuring the organizational chart of the tactical and operational units of the Cameroon Customs administration as illustrated below:

The customs sectors will be changed in regional directorates to ensure more efficiency, harmonization of organization, easier mobility and emphasized specialization. Therefore the proposed configuration looks as follows:

- ➤ There will be 10 regional directorates instead of 12 customs sectors presented as follows: (The regional directorate of littoral, the regional directorate of centre, the regional directorate of south, the regional directorate of east, the regional directorate of adamawa, the regional directorate north, the regional directorate of far north, the regional directorate of north west, the regional directorate of south west and the regional directorate of west).The regional director is the representative of the GM and each strategic director at the regional level.

- ❖ Each regional director who must be senior customs officers having accumulated a minimum of 15 years experience will be assisted by an assistant regional director in charge of personnel and administrative affairs, an assistant regional director in charge of commercial operations, an assistant regional director of statistics and performance and an assistant regional director in charge of surveillance. All must have accumulated a minimum experience of 10 years.

- • The assistant regional director in charge of personnel and administration will be in charge of the management of HR of the regional directorate in coordination with the director of HR; the logistics and budgeting in coordination with the director of supplies and transportation; the mails management of the regional directorate; the communication system of the regional directorate in coordination with the sub director of communication, information and public relations; the audit and internal control in coordination with the director in charge of audit; all administrative affairs of the regional directorate. He will be assisted by 02 sub directors i.e. the sub director of personnel and logistics and the sub director of administrative affairs.

- The sub director of personnel and logistics, who must be specialized in management sciences and having accumulated an experience of 05 years minimum, will be assisted by 02 heads of service i.e. a chief of service of personnel and a chief of service of logistics.

The chief of service of personnel will be in charge of the management of HR of the regional directorate in coordination with the director of HR. In addition to the chief of service who must be specialized in HR, the service will comprise 05 research officers specialists in HR and 01 statistician.

The chief of service of logistics will be in charge of logistics management and budgeting in coordination with the director of supplies and transportation. In addition to the chief of service who must be specialized in logistics and transport, the service will comprise 05 assistant research officers who must be customs officers and 01 statistician.

- The sub director of administrative affairs, who must be specialized in laws and public administration and having accumulated an experience of 05 years minimum, will be assisted by 02 heads of service i.e. a chief of service of communication and information and a chief of service of general affairs.

The chief of service of communication and information will be in charge of the communication system of the regional directorate in coordination with the sub director of communication, information and public relations. In addition to the chief of service who must be specialized in communication, the service will comprise 05 assistant research officers who must be customs officers and 01 statistician.

The chief of service of general affairs will be in charge of the mails management of the regional directorate; the audit and internal control in coordination with the director in charge of audit; all administrative affairs of the regional directorate. In addition to the chief of service who must be specialized in laws and public administration or social sciences, the service will comprise 05 assistant research officers who must be customs officers and 01 statistician.

- The assistant regional director in charge of commercial operations will be assisted by the following sub directors: (the sub director of freight and the sub directors of verifications).The said sub directors must have acquired a minimum of 05 years experience and must be specialized respectively in freight management and customs investigations techniques . Related sciences with the required specializations can be accepted after studies by the HR department in case of absence of such specialists in the organization.

- The sub director of freight will be in charge of the treatment of import/export manifest, the handling and numbering of imported and exported goods. He must specialize in freight management and having acquired a minimum experience of 05 years in the Customs administration. He will be assisted by 02 chiefs of services i.e. the chief of service of treatment of import manifest and the chief of service of export manifest.

The chief of service of import manifest treatment will be in charge of the treatment of import manifests, the exchange of information for the reception of e-manifests and representation of the Customs to the cargo conference and the ecor of imported goods. In addition to the chief of service, the unit will comprise 06 assistant research officers who must be customs officers and 01 statistician.

The chief of service of export manifest treatment will be in charge of the treatment of export manifests and the ecor of exported goods. In addition to the chief of service, the unit will comprise 05 assistant research officers who must be customs officers and 01 statistician.

- The sub directors of verifications and liquidation will be in charge of verifying and calculating the right customs duties to be paid and they will also be in charge of controlling all customs clearing documents, statistics, exploitation, management of litigation cases and related procedures.

We shall distinguish 03 types of sub directorates of verification also referred to as customs houses as follows:

- ✓ 1st class customs houses: Their customs revenues capacities is evaluated as superior to 05 billion monthly;
- ✓ 2nd class customs houses: Their customs revenues capacities is evaluated as from 01 billion monthly to 05 billion monthly;
- ✓ 3rd class customs houses: Their customs revenues capacities are evaluated as less than 01 billion monthly.

The regional directorate of littoral will comprise the following customs houses:

- The littoral air customs house in charge of importation (littoral 1): It will be headed by a sub director who must have an experience of at least 05 years as customs officers. He will be assisted by a chief of service of verification, a chief of service of exploitation and a chief of service of litigation.

  The chief of service of verification who is in charge of following up customs clearing operations and inspection of goods for clearance will be assisted by 10 inspectors having the rank of assistant chiefs of service.

  The chief of service of exploitation will be in charge of the ecor of imported goods by air, the follow up of related statistics, the regularity of air certificates of origin, the clearance of air manifests and licenses as well as the treatment of import manifest through air operations in his customs house; this will be done in collaboration and coordination with the sub director of freight in charge of centralizing all information concerning freight. He will be assisted by 03 assistant research officers and 01 statistician.

  The chief of service of litigation will be in charge of the management of litigation cases in the customs house, the recovery of fines, the management of customs disputes in the customs house, auction sales and the distribution and management of compensations and benefits. He will be assisted by 02 assistant research officers and 01 statistician.

- **The littoral air customs house in charge of exportation (littoral 2):** It will be headed by a sub director who must have an experience of at least 05 years as customs officers. He will be assisted by a chief of service of verification, a chief of service of exploitation and a chief of service of litigation.

  The chief of service of verification who is charge of following up customs clearing operations and inspection of goods for clearance will be assisted by 05 inspectors having the rank of assistant chiefs of service.

  The chief of service of exploitation will be in charge of the ecor of exported goods by air, the follow up of related statistics, the regularity of air certificates of origin, the clearance of air manifests and licenses as well as the treatment of export manifest through air operations in his customs house; this will be done in collaboration and coordination with the sub director of freight in charge of centralizing all information concerning freight. He will be assisted by 02 assistant research officers and 01 statistician.

  The chief of service of litigation will be in charge of the management of litigation cases in the customs house, the recovery of fines, the management of customs disputes in the customs house, auction sales and the distribution and management of compensations and benefits. He will be assisted by 01 assistant research officers and 01 statistician.

- **The littoral air customs house in charge of parcels and mails (littoral 3):** It will be headed by a sub director who must have an experience of at least 05 years as customs officers. He will be assisted by a chief of service of verification, exploitation and litigation for each parcels and mails house.

  The chief of service of verification, exploitation and litigation who is charge of following up customs clearing operations and inspection of goods for clearance, the ecor of goods by air parcels and mails , the follow up of related statistics, the regularity of air certificates of origin, the clearance of air manifests and licenses as well as the treatment of manifest through air parcels and mails operations in his customs house, the management of litigation cases in the customs house, the recovery of fines, the management of customs disputes in the customs house, auction sales and the distribution and management of compensations and benefits will be assisted by 01 inspector having the rank of assistant chiefs of service, 01 statistician and 02 customs agents for manual operations.

- The littoral sea customs house in charge of exportations (littoral 4): It will be headed by a sub director who must have an experience of at least 05 years as customs officers. He will be assisted by a chief of service of verification, a chief of service of exploitation and a chief of service of litigation.

The chief of service of verification who is charge of following up customs clearing operations and inspection of goods for clearance will be assisted by 05 inspectors having the rank of assistant chiefs of service.

The chief of service of exploitation will be in charge of the ecor of exported goods by sea, the follow up of related statistics, the regularity of sea certificates of origin, the clearance of sea manifests and licenses as well as the treatment of export manifest through sea operations in his customs house; this will be done in collaboration and coordination with the sub director of freight in charge of centralizing all information concerning freight. He will be assisted by 02 assistant research officers and 01 statistician.

The chief of service of litigation will be in charge of the management of litigation cases in the customs house, the recovery of fines, the management of customs disputes in the customs house, auction sales and the distribution and management of compensations and benefits. He will be assisted by 01 assistant research officers and 01 statistician.

- The littoral sea customs house in charge of imported vehicles in containers (littoral 5): It will be headed by a sub director who must have an experience of at least 05 years as customs officers. He will be assisted by a chief of service of verification, a chief of service of exploitation and a chief of service of litigation.

The chief of service of verification who is in charge of following up customs clearing operations and inspection of goods for clearance will be assisted by 10 inspectors having the rank of assistant chiefs of service.

The chief of service of exploitation will be in charge of the ecor of imported cars by containers, the follow up of related statistics, the regularity of sea certificates of origin, the clearance of manifests and licenses as well as the treatment of import manifests; this will be done in collaboration and coordination with the sub director of freight in charge of centralizing all information concerning freight. He will be assisted by 03 assistant research officers and 01 statistician.

The chief of service of litigation will be in charge of the management of litigation cases in the customs house, the recovery of fines, the management of customs disputes in the customs house, auction sales and the distribution and management of compensations and benefits. He will be assisted by 02 assistant research officers and 01 statistician.

- <u>The littoral sea customs house in charge of imported vehicles not in containers (littoral 6)</u>: It will be headed by a sub director who must have an experience of at least 05 years as customs officers. He will be assisted by a chief of service of verification, a chief of service of exploitation and a chief of service of litigation.

The chief of service of verification who is in charge of following up customs clearing operations and inspection of goods for clearance will be assisted by 10 inspectors having the rank of assistant chiefs of service.

The chief of service of exploitation will be in charge of the ecor of imported cars not in containers, the follow up of related statistics, the regularity of sea certificates of origin, the clearance of manifests and licenses as well as the treatment of import manifests; this will be done in collaboration and coordination with the sub director of freight in charge of centralizing all information concerning freight. He will be assisted by 03 assistant research officers and 01 statistician.

The chief of service of litigation will be in charge of the management of litigation cases in the customs house, the recovery of fines, the management of customs disputes in the customs house, auction sales and the distribution and

management of compensations and benefits. He will be assisted by 02 assistant research officers and 01 statistician.

- The littoral sea customs house in charge of imported basic necessities or category 1 goods (littoral 7):

It will be headed by a sub director who must have an experience of at least 05 years as customs officers. He will be assisted by a chief of service of verification, a chief of service of exploitation and a chief of service of litigation.

The chief of service of verification who is in charge of following up customs clearing operations and inspection of goods for clearance will be assisted by 10 inspectors having the rank of assistant chiefs of service.

The chief of service of exploitation will be in charge of the ecor of imported cars not in containers, the follow up of related statistics, the regularity of sea certificates of origin, the clearance of manifests and licenses as well as the treatment of import manifests; this will be done in collaboration and coordination with the sub director of freight in charge of centralizing all information concerning freight. He will be assisted by 03 assistant research officers and 01 statistician.

The chief of service of litigation will be in charge of the management of litigation cases in the customs house, the recovery of fines, the management of customs disputes in the customs house, auction sales and the distribution and management of compensations and benefits. He will be assisted by 02 assistant research officers and 01 statistician.

- The littoral sea customs house in charge of imported raw materials and capital goods or category 2 goods (littoral 8): It will be headed by a sub director who must have an experience of at least 05 years as customs officers. He will be assisted by a chief of service of verification, a chief of service of exploitation and a chief of service of litigation.

The chief of service of verification who is in charge of following up customs clearing operations and inspection of goods for clearance will be assisted by 10 inspectors having the rank of assistant chiefs of service.

The chief of service of exploitation will be in charge of the ecor of imported cars not in containers, the follow up of related statistics, the regularity of sea certificates of origin, the clearance of manifests and licenses as well as the treatment of import manifests; this will be done in collaboration and coordination with the sub director of freight in charge of centralizing all information concerning freight. He will be assisted by 03 assistant research officers and 01 statistician.

The chief of service of litigation will be in charge of the management of litigation cases in the customs house, the recovery of fines, the management of customs disputes in the customs house, auction sales and the distribution and management of compensations and benefits. He will be assisted by 02 assistant research officers and 01 statistician.

- The littoral sea customs house in charge of imported intermediate or miscellaneous goods or category 3 goods (littoral 9): It will be headed by a sub director who must have an experience of at least 05 years as customs officers. He will be assisted by a chief of service of verification, a chief of service of exploitation and a chief of service of litigation.

The chief of service of verification who is in charge of following up customs clearing operations and inspection of goods for clearance will be assisted by 10 inspectors having the rank of assistant chiefs of service.

The chief of service of exploitation will be in charge of the ecor of imported cars not in containers, the follow up of related statistics, the regularity of sea certificates of origin, the clearance of manifests and licenses as well as the treatment of import manifests; this will be done in collaboration and coordination with the sub director of freight in charge of centralizing all information concerning freight. He will be assisted by 03 assistant research officers and 01 statistician.

The chief of service of litigation will be in charge of the management of litigation cases in the customs house, the recovery of fines, the management of customs disputes in the customs house, auction sales and the distribution and

management of compensations and benefits. He will be assisted by 02 assistant research officers and 01 statistician.

- The littoral sea customs house in charge of imported consumer goods except cars or category 4 goods (littoral 10): It will be headed by a sub director who must have an experience of at least 05 years as customs officers. He will be assisted by a chief of service of verification, a chief of service of exploitation and a chief of service of litigation.

The chief of service of verification who is in charge of following up customs clearing operations and inspection of goods for clearance will be assisted by 10 inspectors having the rank of assistant chiefs of service.

The chief of service of exploitation will be in charge of the ecor of imported cars not in containers, the follow up of related statistics, the regularity of sea certificates of origin, the clearance of manifests and licenses as well as the treatment of import manifests; this will be done in collaboration and coordination with the sub director of freight in charge of centralizing all information concerning freight. He will be assisted by 03 assistant research officers and 01 statistician.

The chief of service of litigation will be in charge of the management of litigation cases in the customs house, the recovery of fines, the management of customs disputes in the customs house, auction sales and the distribution and management of compensations and benefits. He will be assisted by 02 assistant research officers and 01 statistician.

- The littoral customs house in charge of transit (littoral 11): It will be headed by a sub director who must have an experience of at least 05 years as customs officers. He will be assisted by a chief of service of verification, a chief of service of exploitation and a chief of service of litigation.

The chief of service of verification who is in charge of following up customs clearing operations and inspection of goods for clearance will be assisted by 05 inspectors having the rank of assistant chiefs of service.

The chief of service of exploitation will be in charge of following up cautions fees, their related statistics and the regularity of transit operations. He will be assisted by 03 assistant research officers and 01 statistician.

The chief of service of litigation will be in charge of the management of litigation cases in the customs house, the recovery of fines, the management of customs disputes in the customs house, auction sales and the distribution and management of compensations and benefits. He will be assisted by 02 assistant research officers and 01 statistician.

- The littoral customs house in charge of other suspensive and economic regimes (littoral 12): It will be headed by a sub director who must have an experience of at least 05 years as customs officers. He will be assisted by a chief of service of verification, a chief of service of exploitation and a chief of service of litigation.

The chief of service of verification who is in charge of following up customs clearing operations and inspection of goods for clearance will be assisted by 05 inspectors having the rank of assistant chiefs of service.

The chief of service of exploitation will be in charge of following up cautions fees, their related statistics and the regularity of suspensive and economic regimes operations. He will be assisted by 03 assistant research officers and 01 statistician.

The chief of service of litigation will be in charge of the management of litigation cases in the customs house, the recovery of fines, the management of customs disputes in the customs house, auction sales and the distribution and management of compensations and benefits. He will be assisted by 02 assistant research officers and 01 statistician.

- The littoral customs house in charge of clearance of petroleum products (littoral 13): It will be headed by a sub director who must have an experience of at least 05 years as customs officers. He will be assisted by a chief of service of verification, a chief of service of exploitation and a chief of service of litigation.

The chief of service of verification who is in charge of following up customs clearing operations and inspection of goods for clearance will be assisted by 05 inspectors having the rank of assistant chiefs of service.

The chief of service of exploitation will be in charge of following up cautions fees, their related statistics and the regularity of operations in collaboration with other structures concerned with clearance of petroleum products. He will be assisted by 03 assistant research officers and 01 statistician.

The chief of service of litigation will be in charge of the management of litigation cases in the customs house, the recovery of fines, the management of customs disputes in the customs house, auction sales and the distribution and management of compensations and benefits. He will be assisted by 02 assistant research officers and 01 statistician.

The regional directorate of center will comprise the following customs houses:

- The Center customs house in charge of rail station (Center 1): It will be headed by a sub director who must have an experience of at least 05 years as customs officers. He will be assisted by a chief of service of verification, a chief of service of exploitation and a chief of service of litigation.

The chief of service of verification who is in charge of following up customs clearing operations and inspection of goods for clearance will be assisted by 05 inspectors having the rank of assistant chiefs of service.

The chief of service of exploitation will be in charge of the ecor of imported goods, the follow up of related statistics, the regularity of certificates of origin, the clearance of manifests and licenses as well as the follow up of suspensive and economic regimes. He will be assisted by 04 assistant research officers specialized respectively in the follow up of transit, hydrocarbons, temporary admissions and a last one for other regimes. The service will comprise 01 statistician.

The chief of service of litigation will be in charge of the management of litigation cases in the customs house, the recovery of fines, the management of customs disputes in the customs house, auction sales and the distribution and

management of compensations and benefits. He will be assisted by 02 assistant research officers and 01 statistician.

- The Center customs house in charge of mails and parcels (Center 2): It will be headed by a sub director who must have an experience of at least 05 years as customs officers. He will be assisted by a chief of service of verification, a chief of service of exploitation and a chief of service of litigation.

  The chief of service of verification who is in charge of following up customs clearing operations and inspection of goods for clearance will be assisted by 05 inspectors having the rank of assistant chiefs of service.

  The chief of service of exploitation will be in charge of the ecor of imported goods, the follow up of related statistics, the regularity of certificates of origin, the clearance of manifests and licenses as well as the follow up of suspensive and economic regimes. The service will comprise 01 statistician.

  The chief of service of litigation will be in charge of the management of litigation cases in the customs house, the recovery of fines, the management of customs disputes in the customs house, auction sales and the distribution and management of compensations and benefits. He will be assisted by 02 assistant research officers and 01 statistician.

- The Center customs house in charge of air operations (Center 3): It will be headed by a sub director who must have an experience of at least 05 years as customs officers. He will be assisted by a chief of service of verification, a chief of service of exploitation and a chief of service of litigation.

  The chief of service of verification who is in charge of following up customs clearing operations and inspection of goods for clearance will be assisted by 05 inspectors having the rank of assistant chiefs of service.

  The chief of service of exploitation will be in charge of the ecor of imported goods, the follow up of related statistics, the regularity of certificates of origin, the clearance of manifests and licenses as well as the follow up of suspensive and economic regimes. The service will comprise 01 statistician.

The chief of service of litigation will be in charge of the management of litigation cases in the customs house, the recovery of fines, the management of customs disputes in the customs house, auction sales and the distribution and management of compensations and benefits. He will be assisted by 02 assistant research officers and 01 statistician.

- The Center customs house in charge of external operations (Center 4): It will be headed by a sub director who must have an experience of at least 05 years as customs officers. He will be assisted by a chief of service of verification, a chief of service of exploitation and a chief of service of litigation. It shall be based in mbalmayo and will be competent for any operations carried out of Yaoundé but still in the center region.

The chief of service of verification who is in charge of following up customs clearing operations and inspection of goods for clearance will be assisted by 02 inspectors having the rank of assistant chiefs of service.

The chief of service of exploitation will be in charge of the ecor of goods, the follow up of related statistics, the regularity of certificates of origin, the clearance of manifests and licenses as well as the follow up of suspensive and economic regimes. The service will comprise 01 statistician.

The chief of service of litigation will be in charge of the management of litigation cases in the customs house, the recovery of fines, the management of customs disputes in the customs house, auction sales and the distribution and management of compensations and benefits. He will be assisted by 01 assistant research officers and 01 statistician.

The regional directorate of Adamawa will comprise the following customs houses:

- The Adamawa customs house in charge of rail station (Adamawa 1): It will be headed by a sub director who must have an experience of at least 05 years as customs officers. He will be assisted by a chief of service of verification, a chief of service of exploitation and a chief of service of litigation.

  The chief of service of verification who is in charge of following up customs clearing operations and inspection of goods for clearance will be assisted by 03 inspectors having the rank of assistant chiefs of service.

  The chief of service of exploitation will be in charge of the ecor of imported goods, the follow up of related statistics, the regularity of certificates of origin, the clearance of manifests and licenses as well as the follow up of suspensive and economic regimes. He will be assisted by 04 assistant research officers specialized respectively in the follow up of transit, hydrocarbons, temporary admissions and a last one for other regimes. The service will comprise 01 statistician.

  The chief of service of litigation will be in charge of the management of litigation cases in the customs house, the recovery of fines, the management of customs disputes in the customs house, auction sales and the distribution and management of compensations and benefits. He will be assisted by 02 assistant research officers and 01 statistician.

- The Adamawa customs house in charge of Banyo (Adamawa 2) It will be headed by a sub director who must have an experience of at least 05 years as customs officers. He will be assisted by a chief of service of verification, a chief of service of exploitation and a chief of service of litigation.

  The chief of service of verification who is in charge of following up customs clearing operations and inspection of goods for clearance will be assisted by 03 inspectors having the rank of assistant chiefs of service.

  The chief of service of exploitation will be in charge of the ecor of imported goods, the follow up of related statistics, the regularity of certificates of origin,

the clearance of manifests and licenses as well as the follow up of suspensive and economic regimes. The service will comprise 01 statistician.

The chief of service of litigation will be in charge of the management of litigation cases in the customs house, the recovery of fines, the management of customs disputes in the customs house, auction sales and the distribution and management of compensations and benefits. He will be assisted by 02 assistant research officers and 01 statistician.

- The Adamawa customs house in charge of external operations (Adamawa 3): It will be headed by a sub director who must have an experience of at least 05 years as customs officers. He will be assisted by a chief of service of verification, a chief of service of exploitation and a chief of service of litigation. It will be competent for any operations carried respectively in Bankim, Mayo-Darlé, Meiganga, Tibati, Tignère as well as mails and parcels.

The chief of service of verification who is in charge of following up customs clearing operations and inspection of goods for clearance will be assisted by 06 inspectors having the rank of assistant chiefs of service. Each will be in charge of one locality and will be assisted by one customs agent each. They will be located in the said area.

The chief of service of exploitation will be in charge of the ecor of goods, the follow up of related statistics, the regularity of certificates of origin, the clearance of manifests and licenses as well as the follow up of suspensive and economic regimes. The service will comprise 01 statistician.

The chief of service of litigation will be in charge of the management of litigation cases in the customs house, the recovery of fines, the management of customs disputes in the customs house, auction sales and the distribution and management of compensations and benefits. He will be assisted by 01 assistant research officers and 01 statistician.

The regional directorate of East will comprise the following customs houses:

- <u>The East customs house in charge of Bertoua operations (East 1)</u>: It will be headed by a sub director who must have an experience of at least 05 years as customs officers. He will be assisted by a chief of service of verification, a chief of service of exploitation and a chief of service of litigation.

  The chief of service of verification who is in charge of following up customs clearing operations and inspection of goods for clearance will be assisted by 03 inspectors having the rank of assistant chiefs of service.

  The chief of service of exploitation will be in charge of the ecor of imported goods, the follow up of related statistics, the regularity of certificates of origin, the clearance of manifests and licenses as well as the follow up of suspensive and economic regimes. The service will comprise 01 statistician.

  The chief of service of litigation will be in charge of the management of litigation cases in the customs house, the recovery of fines, the management of customs disputes in the customs house, auction sales and the distribution and management of compensations and benefits. He will be assisted by 02 assistant research officers and 01 statistician.

- <u>The East customs house in charge of Belabo operations (East 2)</u>: It will be headed by a sub director who must have an experience of at least 05 years as customs officers. He will be assisted by a chief of service of verification, a chief of service of exploitation and a chief of service of litigation.

  The chief of service of verification who is in charge of following up customs clearing operations and inspection of goods for clearance will be assisted by 03 inspectors having the rank of assistant chiefs of service.

  The chief of service of exploitation will be in charge of the ecor of imported goods, the follow up of related statistics, the regularity of certificates of origin, the clearance of manifests and licenses as well as the follow up of suspensive and economic regimes. The service will comprise 01 statistician.

The chief of service of litigation will be in charge of the management of litigation cases in the customs house, the recovery of fines, the management of customs disputes in the customs house, auction sales and the distribution and management of compensations and benefits. He will be assisted by 02 assistant research officers and 01 statistician.

- <u>The East customs house in charge of mails and parcels (East 3)</u>: It will be headed by a sub director who must have an experience of at least 05 years as customs officers. He will be assisted by a chief of service of verification, a chief of service of exploitation and a chief of service of litigation.

The chief of service of verification who is in charge of following up customs clearing operations and inspection of goods for clearance will be assisted by 01 inspector having the rank of assistant chiefs of service.

The chief of service of exploitation will be in charge of the ecor of imported goods, the follow up of related statistics, the regularity of certificates of origin, the clearance of manifests and licenses as well as the follow up of suspensive and economic regimes. The service will comprise 01 statistician.

The chief of service of litigation will be in charge of the management of litigation cases in the customs house, the recovery of fines, the management of customs disputes in the customs house, auction sales and the distribution and management of compensations and benefits. He will be assisted by 01 assistant research officers and 01 statistician.

- <u>The East customs house in charge of external operations (East 4)</u>: It will be headed by a sub director who must have an experience of at least 05 years as customs officers. He will be assisted by a chief of service of verification, a chief of service of exploitation and a chief of service of litigation. It will be competent for any operations carried respectively in Kentzou and Ntam or any other locality found out of Bertoua

The chief of service of verification who is in charge of following up customs clearing operations and inspection of goods for clearance will be assisted by 02 inspectors having the rank of assistant chiefs of service. Each will be in charge of one locality and will be assisted by one customs agent each. They will be located in the said area.

The chief of service of exploitation will be in charge of the ecor of goods, the follow up of related statistics, the regularity of certificates of origin, the clearance of manifests and licenses as well as the follow up of suspensive and economic regimes. The service will comprise 01 statistician.

The chief of service of litigation will be in charge of the management of litigation cases in the customs house, the recovery of fines, the management of customs disputes in the customs house, auction sales and the distribution and management of compensations and benefits. He will be assisted by 01 assistant research officers and 01 statistician.

The regional directorate of Far North will comprise the following customs houses:

- The Far North customs house in charge of Maroua operations (Far North 1): It will be headed by a sub director who must have an experience of at least 05 years as customs officers. He will be assisted by a chief of service of verification, a chief of service of exploitation and a chief of service of litigation.

The chief of service of verification who is in charge of following up customs clearing operations and inspection of goods for clearance will be assisted by 03 inspectors having the rank of assistant chiefs of service.

The chief of service of exploitation will be in charge of the ecor of imported goods, the follow up of related statistics, the regularity of certificates of origin, the clearance of manifests and licenses as well as the follow up of suspensive and economic regimes. The service will comprise 01 statistician.

The chief of service of litigation will be in charge of the management of litigation cases in the customs house, the recovery of fines, the management of customs disputes in the customs house, auction sales and the distribution and management of compensations and benefits. He will be assisted by 02 assistant research officers and 01 statistician.

- The Far North customs house in charge of Limani operations (Far North 2): It will be headed by a sub director who must have an experience of at least 05 years as customs officers. He will be assisted by a chief of service of verification, a chief of service of exploitation and a chief of service of litigation.

The chief of service of verification who is in charge of following up customs clearing operations and inspection of goods for clearance will be assisted by 03 inspectors having the rank of assistant chiefs of service.

The chief of service of exploitation will be in charge of the ecor of imported goods, the follow up of related statistics, the regularity of certificates of origin, the clearance of manifests and licenses as well as the follow up of suspensive and economic regimes. The service will comprise 01 statistician.

The chief of service of litigation will be in charge of the management of litigation cases in the customs house, the recovery of fines, the management of customs disputes in the customs house, auction sales and the distribution and management of compensations and benefits. He will be assisted by 02 assistant research officers and 01 statistician.

- The Far North customs house in charge of Kousséri operations (Far North 3): It will be headed by a sub director who must have an experience of at least 05 years as customs officers. He will be assisted by a chief of service of verification, a chief of service of exploitation and a chief of service of litigation.

The chief of service of verification who is in charge of following up customs clearing operations and inspection of goods for clearance will be assisted by 03 inspectors having the rank of assistant chiefs of service.

The chief of service of exploitation will be in charge of the ecor of imported goods, the follow up of related statistics, the regularity of certificates of origin, the clearance of manifests and licenses as well as the follow up of suspensive and economic regimes. The service will comprise 01 statistician.

The chief of service of litigation will be in charge of the management of litigation cases in the customs house, the recovery of fines, the management of customs disputes in the customs house, auction sales and the distribution and management of compensations and benefits. He will be assisted by 02 assistant research officers and 01 statistician.

- The Far North customs house in charge of Fotokol operations (Far North 4): It will be headed by a sub director who must have an experience of at least 05 years as customs officers. He will be assisted by a chief of service of verification, a chief of service of exploitation and a chief of service of litigation.

The chief of service of verification who is in charge of following up customs clearing operations and inspection of goods for clearance will be assisted by 03 inspectors having the rank of assistant chiefs of service.

The chief of service of exploitation will be in charge of the ecor of imported goods, the follow up of related statistics, the regularity of certificates of origin, the clearance of manifests and licenses as well as the follow up of suspensive and economic regimes. The service will comprise 01 statistician.

The chief of service of litigation will be in charge of the management of litigation cases in the customs house, the recovery of fines, the management of customs disputes in the customs house, auction sales and the distribution and management of compensations and benefits. He will be assisted by 02 assistant research officers and 01 statistician.

- The Far North customs house in charge of mails and parcels (Far North 5): It will be headed by a sub director who must have an experience of at least 05 years as customs officers. He will be assisted by a chief of service of verification, a chief of service of exploitation and a chief of service of litigation.

The chief of service of verification who is in charge of following up customs clearing operations and inspection of goods for clearance will be assisted by 01 inspector having the rank of assistant chiefs of service.

The chief of service of exploitation will be in charge of the ecor of imported goods, the follow up of related statistics, the regularity of certificates of origin,

the clearance of manifests and licenses as well as the follow up of suspensive and economic regimes. The service will comprise 01 statistician.

The chief of service of litigation will be in charge of the management of litigation cases in the customs house, the recovery of fines, the management of customs disputes in the customs house, auction sales and the distribution and management of compensations and benefits. He will be assisted by 01 assistant research officers and 01 statistician.

- The Far North customs house in charge of external operations (Far North 6): It will be headed by a sub director who must have an experience of at least 05 years as customs officers. He will be assisted by a chief of service of verification, a chief of service of exploitation and a chief of service of litigation. It will be competent for any operations carried respectively Bangoua, Bourha, Dabanga, Goulfey, Mblamé, Kolofata, Koza, Mokolo, Waza, Yagoua and any other surrounding locality (ies).

The chief of service of verification who is in charge of following up customs clearing operations and inspection of goods for clearance will be assisted by 10 inspectors having the rank of assistant chiefs of service. Each will be in charge of one locality and will be assisted by one customs agent each. They will be located in the said area.

The chief of service of exploitation will be in charge of the ecor of goods, the follow up of related statistics, the regularity of certificates of origin, the clearance of manifests and licenses as well as the follow up of suspensive and economic regimes. The service will comprise 01 statistician.

The chief of service of litigation will be in charge of the management of litigation cases in the customs house, the recovery of fines, the management of customs disputes in the customs house, auction sales and the distribution and management of compensations and benefits. He will be assisted by 01 assistant research officers and 01 statistician.

The regional directorate of North will comprise the following customs houses:

- The North customs house in charge of Garoua operations (North 1): It will be headed by a sub director who must have an experience of at least 05 years as customs officers. He will be assisted by a chief of service of verification, a chief of service of exploitation and a chief of service of litigation.

  The chief of service of verification who is in charge of following up customs clearing operations and inspection of goods for clearance will be assisted by 03 inspectors having the rank of assistant chiefs of service.

  The chief of service of exploitation will be in charge of the ecor of imported goods, the follow up of related statistics, the regularity of certificates of origin, the clearance of manifests and licenses as well as the follow up of suspensive and economic regimes. The service will comprise 01 statistician.

  The chief of service of litigation will be in charge of the management of litigation cases in the customs house, the recovery of fines, the management of customs disputes in the customs house, auction sales and the distribution and management of compensations and benefits. He will be assisted by 02 assistant research officers and 01 statistician.

- The North customs house in charge of Gashiga operations (North 2): It will be headed by a sub director who must have an experience of at least 05 years as customs officers. He will be assisted by a chief of service of verification, a chief of service of exploitation and a chief of service of litigation.

  The chief of service of verification who is in charge of following up customs clearing operations and inspection of goods for clearance will be assisted by 03 inspectors having the rank of assistant chiefs of service.

  The chief of service of exploitation will be in charge of the ecor of imported goods, the follow up of related statistics, the regularity of certificates of origin, the clearance of manifests and licenses as well as the follow up of suspensive and economic regimes. The service will comprise 01 statistician.

  The chief of service of litigation will be in charge of the management of litigation cases in the customs house, the recovery of fines, the management of customs disputes in the customs house, auction sales and the distribution and management of compensations and benefits. He will be assisted by 02 assistant research officers and 01 statistician.

- The North customs house in charge of Dourbeye operations (North 3): It will be headed by a sub director who must have an experience of at least 05 years as customs officers. He will be assisted by a chief of service of verification, a chief of service of exploitation and a chief of service of litigation.

  The chief of service of verification who is in charge of following up customs clearing operations and inspection of goods for clearance will be assisted by 03 inspectors having the rank of assistant chiefs of service.

  The chief of service of exploitation will be in charge of the ecor of imported goods, the follow up of related statistics, the regularity of certificates of origin, the clearance of manifests and licenses as well as the follow up of suspensive and economic regimes. The service will comprise 01 statistician.

  The chief of service of litigation will be in charge of the management of litigation cases in the customs house, the recovery of fines, the management of customs disputes in the customs house, auction sales and the distribution and

management of compensations and benefits. He will be assisted by 02 assistant research officers and 01 statistician.

- The North customs house in charge of Garoua air operations (North 4): It will be headed by a sub director who must have an experience of at least 05 years as customs officers. He will be assisted by a chief of service of verification, a chief of service of exploitation and a chief of service of litigation.

The chief of service of verification who is in charge of following up customs clearing operations and inspection of goods for clearance will be assisted by 02 inspectors having the rank of assistant chiefs of service.

The chief of service of exploitation will be in charge of the ecor of imported goods, the follow up of related statistics, the regularity of certificates of origin, the clearance of manifests and licenses as well as the follow up of suspensive and economic regimes. The service will comprise 01 statistician.

The chief of service of litigation will be in charge of the management of litigation cases in the customs house, the recovery of fines, the management of customs disputes in the customs house, auction sales and the distribution and management of compensations and benefits. He will be assisted by 01 assistant research officers and 01 statistician.

- The North customs house in charge of Garoua mails and parcels operations (North 5): It will be headed by a sub director who must have an experience of at least 05 years as customs officers. He will be assisted by a chief of service of verification, a chief of service of exploitation and a chief of service of litigation.

The chief of service of verification who is in charge of following up customs clearing operations and inspection of goods for clearance will be assisted by 02 inspectors having the rank of assistant chiefs of service.

The chief of service of exploitation will be in charge of the ecor of imported goods, the follow up of related statistics, the regularity of certificates of origin, the clearance of manifests and licenses as well as the follow up of suspensive and economic regimes. The service will comprise 01 statistician.

The chief of service of litigation will be in charge of the management of litigation cases in the customs house, the recovery of fines, the management of customs disputes in the customs house, auction sales and the distribution and management of compensations and benefits. He will be assisted by 01 assistant research officers and 01 statistician.

- The North customs house in charge of external operations (North 6): It will be headed by a sub director who must have an experience of at least 05 years as customs officers. He will be assisted by a chief of service of verification, a chief of service of exploitation and a chief of service of litigation. It will be competent for any operations carried out respectively in Bandake, Figuil, Lagdo, Touroua, Rey Bouba and Touboro.

The chief of service of verification who is in charge of following up customs clearing operations and inspection of goods for clearance will be assisted by 06 inspectors having the rank of assistant chiefs of service. Each will be in charge of one locality and will be assisted by one customs agent each. They will be located in the said area.

The chief of service of exploitation will be in charge of the ecor of goods, the follow up of related statistics, the regularity of certificates of origin, the clearance of manifests and licenses as well as the follow up of suspensive and economic regimes. The service will comprise 01 statistician.

The chief of service of litigation will be in charge of the management of litigation cases in the customs house, the recovery of fines, the management of customs disputes in the customs house, auction sales and the distribution and management of compensations and benefits. He will be assisted by 01 assistant research officers and 01 statistician.

The regional directorate of South will comprise the following customs houses:

- The South customs house in charge of Ebolowa operations (South 1): It will be headed by a sub director who must have an experience of at least 05 years as customs officers. He will be assisted by a chief of service of verification, a chief of service of exploitation and a chief of service of litigation.

77

The chief of service of verification who is in charge of following up customs clearing operations and inspection of goods for clearance will be assisted by 02 inspectors having the rank of assistant chiefs of service.

The chief of service of exploitation will be in charge of the ecor of imported goods, the follow up of related statistics, the regularity of certificates of origin, the clearance of manifests and licenses as well as the follow up of suspensive and economic regimes. The service will comprise 01 statistician.

The chief of service of litigation will be in charge of the management of litigation cases in the customs house, the recovery of fines, the management of customs disputes in the customs house, auction sales and the distribution and management of compensations and benefits. He will be assisted by 01 assistant research officers and 01 statistician.

- The South customs house in charge of Ambam operations (South 2): It will be headed by a sub director who must have an experience of at least 05 years as customs officers. He will be assisted by a chief of service of verification, a chief of service of exploitation and a chief of service of litigation.

The chief of service of verification who is in charge of following up customs clearing operations and inspection of goods for clearance will be assisted by 02 inspectors having the rank of assistant chiefs of service.

The chief of service of exploitation will be in charge of the ecor of imported goods, the follow up of related statistics, the regularity of certificates of origin, the clearance of manifests and licenses as well as the follow up of suspensive and economic regimes. The service will comprise 01 statistician.

The chief of service of litigation will be in charge of the management of litigation cases in the customs house, the recovery of fines, the management of customs disputes in the customs house, auction sales and the distribution and management of compensations and benefits. He will be assisted by 01 assistant research officers and 01 statistician.

- The South customs house in charge of Kribi importations operations (South 3): It will be headed by a sub director who must have an experience of at least 05 years as customs officers. He will be assisted by a chief of service of verification, a chief of service of exploitation and a chief of service of litigation.

The chief of service of verification who is in charge of following up customs clearing operations and inspection of goods for clearance will be assisted by 05 inspectors having the rank of assistant chiefs of service.

The chief of service of exploitation will be in charge of the ecor of imported goods, the follow up of related statistics, the regularity of certificates of origin, the clearance of manifests and licenses. The service will comprise 01 statistician.

The chief of service of litigation will be in charge of the management of litigation cases in the customs house, the recovery of fines, the management of customs disputes in the customs house, auction sales and the distribution and management of compensations and benefits. He will be assisted by 02 assistant research officers and 01 statistician.

- The South customs house in charge of Kribi exportations operations (South 4): It will be headed by a sub director who must have an experience of at least 05 years as customs officers. He will be assisted by a chief of service of verification, a chief of service of exploitation and a chief of service of litigation.

The chief of service of verification who is in charge of following up customs clearing operations and inspection of goods for clearance will be assisted by 03 inspectors having the rank of assistant chiefs of service.

The chief of service of exploitation will be in charge of the ecor of imported goods, the follow up of related statistics, the regularity of certificates of origin and the clearance of manifests. The service will comprise 01 statistician.

The chief of service of litigation will be in charge of the management of litigation cases in the customs house, the recovery of fines, the management of customs disputes in the customs house, auction sales and the distribution and management of compensations and benefits. He will be assisted by 02 assistant research officers and 01 statistician.

- The South customs house in charge of Kribi suspensive and economic regimes (South 5): It will be headed by a sub director who must have an experience of at least 05 years as customs officers. He will be assisted by a chief of service of verification, a chief of service of exploitation and a chief of service of litigation.

The chief of service of verification who is in charge of following up customs clearing operations and inspection of goods for clearance will be assisted by 05 inspectors having the rank of assistant chiefs of service.

The chief of service of exploitation will be in charge of following up cautions fees, their related statistics and the regularity of suspensive and economic regimes operations. He will be assisted by 03 assistant research officers and 01 statistician.

The chief of service of litigation will be in charge of the management of litigation cases in the customs house, the recovery of fines, the management of customs disputes in the customs house, auction sales and the distribution and management of compensations and benefits. He will be assisted by 02 assistant research officers and 01 statistician.

The regional directorate of North-West will comprise the following customs houses:

- The North West customs house in charge of Bamenda operations (North West 1): It will be headed by a sub director who must have an experience of at least 05 years as customs officers. He will be assisted by a chief of service of verification, a chief of service of exploitation and a chief of service of litigation.

The chief of service of verification who is in charge of following up customs clearing operations and inspection of goods for clearance will be assisted by 02 inspectors having the rank of assistant chiefs of service.

The chief of service of exploitation will be in charge of the ecor of imported goods, the follow up of related statistics, the regularity of certificates of origin, the clearance of manifests and licenses as well as the follow up of suspensive and economic regimes. The service will comprise 01 statistician.

The chief of service of litigation will be in charge of the management of litigation cases in the customs house, the recovery of fines, the management of customs disputes in the customs house, auction sales and the distribution and management of compensations and benefits. He will be assisted by 01 assistant research officers and 01 statistician.

- The North West customs house in charge of External operations (North West 2): It will be headed by a sub director who must have an experience of at least 05 years as customs officers. He will be assisted by a chief of service of verification, a chief of service of exploitation and a chief of service of litigation. It will be competent for any operations carried respectively in Abuenshie, Essimbi, Yang, Nkambe, Esu, Kumbo, Mwa and Sebongari.

The chief of service of verification who is in charge of following up customs clearing operations and inspection of goods for clearance will be assisted by 08 inspectors having the rank of assistant chiefs of service. Each will be in charge of one locality and will be assisted by one customs agent each. They will be located in the said area.

The chief of service of exploitation will be in charge of the ecor of goods, the follow up of related statistics, the regularity of certificates of origin, the clearance of manifests and licenses as well as the follow up of suspensive and economic regimes. The service will comprise 01 statistician.

The chief of service of litigation will be in charge of the management of litigation cases in the customs house, the recovery of fines, the management of customs disputes in the customs house, auction sales and the distribution and management of compensations and benefits. He will be assisted by 01 assistant research officers and 01 statistician.

The regional directorate of West will comprise the following customs houses:

- The West customs house in charge of Baffoussam operations (West 1): It will be headed by a sub director who must have an experience of at least 05 years as customs officers. He will be assisted by a chief of service of verification, a chief of service of exploitation and a chief of service of litigation.

The chief of service of verification who is in charge of following up customs clearing operations and inspection of goods for clearance will be assisted by 02 inspectors having the rank of assistant chiefs of service.

The chief of service of exploitation will be in charge of the ecor of imported goods, the follow up of related statistics, the regularity of certificates of origin, the clearance of manifests and licenses as well as the follow up of suspensive and economic regimes. The service will comprise 01 statistician.

The chief of service of litigation will be in charge of the management of litigation cases in the customs house, the recovery of fines, the management of customs disputes in the customs house, auction sales and the distribution and management of compensations and benefits. He will be assisted by 01 assistant research officers and 01 statistician.

- The West customs house in charge of External operations (West 2): It will be headed by a sub director who must have an experience of at least 05 years as customs officers. He will be assisted by a chief of service of verification, a chief of service of exploitation and a chief of service of litigation. It will be competent for any operations carried respectively in Dschang, Mbouda and Magda.

The chief of service of verification who is in charge of following up customs clearing operations and inspection of goods for clearance will be assisted by 03 inspectors having the rank of assistant chiefs of service. Each will be in charge of one locality and will be assisted by one customs agent each. They will be located in the said area.

The chief of service of exploitation will be in charge of the ecor of goods, the follow up of related statistics, the regularity of certificates of origin, the clearance of manifests and licenses as well as the follow up of suspensive and economic regimes. The service will comprise 01 statistician.

The chief of service of litigation will be in charge of the management of litigation cases in the customs house, the recovery of fines, the management of customs disputes in the customs house, auction sales and the distribution and

management of compensations and benefits. He will be assisted by 01 assistant research officers and 01 statistician.

The regional directorate of South-West will comprise the following customs houses:

- <u>The South West customs house in charge of Limbe operations (South West 1)</u>: It will be headed by a sub director who must have an experience of at least 05 years as customs officers. He will be assisted by a chief of service of verification, a chief of service of exploitation and a chief of service of litigation.

  The chief of service of verification who is in charge of following up customs clearing operations and inspection of goods for clearance will be assisted by 02 inspectors having the rank of assistant chiefs of service.

  The chief of service of exploitation will be in charge of the ecor of imported goods, the follow up of related statistics, the regularity of certificates of origin, the clearance of manifests and licenses as well as the follow up of suspensive and economic regimes. The service will comprise 01 statistician.

  The chief of service of litigation will be in charge of the management of litigation cases in the customs house, the recovery of fines, the management of customs disputes in the customs house, auction sales and the distribution and management of compensations and benefits. He will be assisted by 01 assistant research officers and 01 statistician.

- <u>The South West customs house in charge of Ekok operations (South West 2)</u>: It will be headed by a sub director who must have an experience of at least 05 years as customs officers. He will be assisted by a chief of service of verification, a chief of service of exploitation and a chief of service of litigation.

  The chief of service of verification who is in charge of following up customs clearing operations and inspection of goods for clearance will be assisted by 02 inspectors having the rank of assistant chiefs of service.

  The chief of service of exploitation will be in charge of the ecor of imported goods, the follow up of related statistics, the regularity of certificates of origin,

the clearance of manifests and licenses as well as the follow up of suspensive and economic regimes. The service will comprise 01 statistician.

The chief of service of litigation will be in charge of the management of litigation cases in the customs house, the recovery of fines, the management of customs disputes in the customs house, auction sales and the distribution and management of compensations and benefits. He will be assisted by 01 assistant research officers and 01 statistician.

- The South West customs house in charge of Kumba operations (South West 3): It will be headed by a sub director who must have an experience of at least 05 years as customs officers. He will be assisted by a chief of service of verification, a chief of service of exploitation and a chief of service of litigation.

The chief of service of verification who is in charge of following up customs clearing operations and inspection of goods for clearance will be assisted by 02 inspectors having the rank of assistant chiefs of service.

The chief of service of exploitation will be in charge of the ecor of imported goods, the follow up of related statistics, the regularity of certificates of origin, the clearance of manifests and licenses as well as the follow up of suspensive and economic regimes. The service will comprise 01 statistician.

The chief of service of litigation will be in charge of the management of litigation cases in the customs house, the recovery of fines, the management of customs disputes in the customs house, auction sales and the distribution and management of compensations and benefits. He will be assisted by 01 assistant research officers and 01 statistician.

- The South West customs house in charge of Mamfé operations (South West 4): It will be headed by a sub director who must have an experience of at least 05 years as customs officers. He will be assisted by a chief of service of verification, a chief of service of exploitation and a chief of service of litigation.

The chief of service of verification who is in charge of following up customs clearing operations and inspection of goods for clearance will be assisted by 02 inspectors having the rank of assistant chiefs of service.

The chief of service of exploitation will be in charge of the ecor of imported goods, the follow up of related statistics, the regularity of certificates of origin, the clearance of manifests and licenses as well as the follow up of suspensive and economic regimes. The service will comprise 01 statistician.

The chief of service of litigation will be in charge of the management of litigation cases in the customs house, the recovery of fines, the management of customs disputes in the customs house, auction sales and the distribution and management of compensations and benefits. He will be assisted by 01 assistant research officers and 01 statistician.

- The South West customs house in charge of Lobe operations (South West 5): It will be headed by a sub director who must have an experience of at least 05 years as customs officers. He will be assisted by a chief of service of verification, a chief of service of exploitation and a chief of service of litigation.

The chief of service of verification who is in charge of following up customs clearing operations and inspection of goods for clearance will be assisted by 02 inspectors having the rank of assistant chiefs of service.

The chief of service of exploitation will be in charge of the ecor of imported goods, the follow up of related statistics, the regularity of certificates of origin, the clearance of manifests and licenses as well as the follow up of suspensive and economic regimes. The service will comprise 01 statistician.

The chief of service of litigation will be in charge of the management of litigation cases in the customs house, the recovery of fines, the management of customs disputes in the customs house, auction sales and the distribution and management of compensations and benefits. He will be assisted by 01 assistant research officers and 01 statistician.

- The South West customs house in charge of Mbonge operations (South West 6): It will be headed by a sub director who must have an experience of at least 05 years as customs officers. He will be assisted by a chief of service of verification, a chief of service of exploitation and a chief of service of litigation.

The chief of service of verification who is in charge of following up customs clearing operations and inspection of goods for clearance will be assisted by 02 inspectors having the rank of assistant chiefs of service.

The chief of service of exploitation will be in charge of the ecor of imported goods, the follow up of related statistics, the regularity of certificates of origin, the clearance of manifests and licenses as well as the follow up of suspensive and economic regimes. The service will comprise 01 statistician.

The chief of service of litigation will be in charge of the management of litigation cases in the customs house, the recovery of fines, the management of customs disputes in the customs house, auction sales and the distribution and management of compensations and benefits. He will be assisted by 01 assistant research officers and 01 statistician.

- The South West customs house in charge of Cap limboh operations (South West 7): It will be headed by a sub director who must have an experience of at least 05 years as customs officers. He will be assisted by a chief of service of verification, a chief of service of exploitation and a chief of service of litigation.

The chief of service of verification who is in charge of following up customs clearing operations and inspection of goods for clearance will be assisted by 02 inspectors having the rank of assistant chiefs of service.

The chief of service of exploitation will be in charge of the ecor of imported goods, the follow up of related statistics, the regularity of certificates of origin, the clearance of manifests and licenses as well as the follow up of suspensive and economic regimes. The service will comprise 01 statistician.

The chief of service of litigation will be in charge of the management of litigation cases in the customs house, the recovery of fines, the management of customs disputes in the customs house, auction sales and the distribution and management of compensations and benefits. He will be assisted by 01 assistant research officers and 01 statistician.

- The South West customs house in charge of Idenau operations (South West 8): It will be headed by a sub director who must have an experience of at least 05 years as customs officers. He will be assisted by a chief of service of verification, a chief of service of exploitation and a chief of service of litigation.

The chief of service of verification who is in charge of following up customs clearing operations and inspection of goods for clearance will be assisted by 02 inspectors having the rank of assistant chiefs of service.

The chief of service of exploitation will be in charge of the ecor of imported goods, the follow up of related statistics, the regularity of certificates of origin, the clearance of manifests and licenses as well as the follow up of suspensive and economic regimes. The service will comprise 01 statistician.

The chief of service of litigation will be in charge of the management of litigation cases in the customs house, the recovery of fines, the management of customs disputes in the customs house, auction sales and the distribution and management of compensations and benefits. He will be assisted by 01 assistant research officers and 01 statistician.

- The South West customs house in charge of Tiko operations (South West 9): It will be headed by a sub director who must have an experience of at least 05 years as customs officers. He will be assisted by a chief of service of verification, a chief of service of exploitation and a chief of service of litigation.

The chief of service of verification who is in charge of following up customs clearing operations and inspection of goods for clearance will be assisted by 02 inspectors having the rank of assistant chiefs of service.

The chief of service of exploitation will be in charge of the ecor of imported goods, the follow up of related statistics, the regularity of certificates of origin, the clearance of manifests and licenses as well as the follow up of suspensive and economic regimes. The service will comprise 01 statistician.

The chief of service of litigation will be in charge of the management of litigation cases in the customs house, the recovery of fines, the management of customs disputes in the customs house, auction sales and the distribution and management of compensations and benefits. He will be assisted by 01 assistant research officers and 01 statistician.

- <u>The South West customs house in charge of External operations (South West 10)</u>: It will be headed by a sub director who must have an experience of at least 05 years as customs officers. He will be assisted by a chief of service of verification, a chief of service of exploitation and a chief of service of litigation. It will be competent for any operations carried respectively in Akwa, Bamousso, Bekoumou, Idabato and Otu.

  The chief of service of verification who is in charge of following up customs clearing operations and inspection of goods for clearance will be assisted by 05 inspectors having the rank of assistant chiefs of service. Each will be in charge of one locality and will be assisted by one customs agent each. They will be located in the said area.

  The chief of service of exploitation will be in charge of the ecor of goods, the follow up of related statistics, the regularity of certificates of origin, the clearance of manifests and licenses as well as the follow up of suspensive and economic regimes. The service will comprise 01 statistician.

  The chief of service of litigation will be in charge of the management of litigation cases in the customs house, the recovery of fines, the management of customs disputes in the customs house, auction sales and the distribution and management of compensations and benefits. He will be assisted by 01 assistant research officers and 01 statistician.

➢ <u>The assistant regional director in charge of surveillance</u>: He will be in charge at the regional level under the coordination of the director of surveillance of : Reporting, data accumulation, collecting the data, data analysis, fighting against fraud , smuggling, counterfeiting; the surveillance of waters, air and lands borders in collaboration with the operational units of regional sectors of Customs administration, controlling the pentiere, protecting sensitive areas, the management of weapons belonging to the Customs' administration and the follow up of air, land and sea logistics relating to the surveillance system, the follow up of paramilitary activities and coordination of march past by customs agents. He must be a senior customs officer having acquired a minimum of 10 years experience and must have carried out specialized training in the domains of surveillance. As close collaborators, he will be assisted by another senior customs officer having acquired a minimum experience of 06 years, having carried out specialized training in the domains of surveillance and 06 research assistants specialized in statistics, reporting, surveillance, smuggling and counterfeiting and customs information.

The assistant regional directors in charge of surveillance will be assisted by the following sub directors and chief of services as illustrated below:

- For the littoral region:

The littoral region will be constituted by the following sub-directors:

1. The littoral customs sub directorate in charge of air surveillance (littoral Zone A): It will be headed by a sub director who must have an experience of at least 05 years as customs officers. He will be assisted by chiefs of services in charge of importations by air; exportations by air; parcels and mails operations.

The chief of service of importations by air will be in charge of the following subunits and missions: surveillance of terminals, boarding of planes, controls of goods removals, delivering outing certificates, and management of customs warehouses located in the airport as well as control of all forms of passengers trafficking in collaboration with other relevant units. It will comprise in addition to the head of unit, 30 customs agents trained in air surveillance methods i.e. 05 per unit plus 01 statistician and 01 IT expert.

The chief of service of exportations by air will be in charge of the following subunits and missions: surveillance of terminals, boarding of planes, controls of goods handling, delivering relevant export customs certificates in collaboration with competent units, management of customs warehouses located in the airport as well as control of all forms of trafficking in collaboration with other relevant units. It will comprise in addition to the head of unit, 18 customs agents trained in air surveillance methods i.e. 03 per unit plus 01 statistician and 01 IT expert.

The chief of service of parcels and mails operations will be in charge of the following subunits and missions: controls of goods handling, delivering relevant export customs certificates in collaboration with competent units, It will comprise in addition to the head of unit, 06 customs agents trained in parcels and mails methods i.e. 02 per unit plus 01 statistician and 01 IT expert.

2. The littoral customs sub directorate in charge of sea surveillance (littoral Zone B): It will be headed by a sub director who must have an experience of at least 05 years as customs officers. He will be assisted by chiefs of services in charge of exportations by sea; imported vehicles by containers; imported vehicles not in containers; imported goods by container ; imported goods not in containers.

The chief of service of exportations by sea will be in charge of the following subunits and missions: controls of goods handling, delivering relevant export customs certificates in collaboration with competent units, management of customs warehouses located in the seaport as well as control of all forms of trafficking in collaboration with other relevant units. It will comprise in addition to the head of unit, 20 customs agents trained in sea operations surveillance methods i.e. 05 per units plus 01 statistician and 01 IT expert.

The chief of service of imported vehicles by container will be in charge of the following subunits and missions: surveillance of terminals, boarding of boats, controls of goods handling, delivering relevant customs certificates in collaboration with competent units, management of customs warehouses as well as control of all forms of trafficking in collaboration with other relevant units. It will comprise in addition to the head of unit, 18 customs agents trained in sea operations surveillance methods i.e. 03 per units plus 01 statistician and 01 IT expert.

The chief of service of imported vehicles not by container will be in charge of the following subunits and missions: surveillance of terminals, boarding of boats, controls of goods handling, delivering relevant customs certificates in collaboration with competent units, management of customs warehouses as well as control of all forms of trafficking in collaboration with other relevant units. It will comprise in addition to the head of unit, 18 customs agents trained in sea operations surveillance methods i.e. 03 per units plus 01 statistician and 01 IT expert.

The chief of service of other imported goods by container will be in charge of the following subunits and missions: surveillance of terminals, boarding of boats, controls of goods handling, delivering relevant customs certificates in collaboration with competent units, management of customs warehouses as well as control of all forms of trafficking in collaboration with other relevant units. It will comprise in addition to the head of unit, 18 customs agents trained in sea operations surveillance methods i.e. 03 per units plus 01 statistician and 01 IT expert.

The chief of service of imported goods not in containers will be in charge of the following subunits and missions: surveillance of terminals, boarding of boats, controls of goods handling, delivering relevant customs certificates in collaboration with competent units, management of customs warehouses as well as control of all forms of trafficking in collaboration with other relevant units. It will comprise in addition to the head of unit, 18 customs agents trained in sea operations surveillance methods i.e. 03 per units plus 01 statistician and 01 IT expert.

3. The littoral customs sub directorate in charge of land surveillance (littoral Zone C): It will be headed by a sub director who must have an experience of at least 05 years as customs officers. He will be assisted by chiefs of services, each in charge of each administrative subdivision of the littoral region i.e. Moungo; Nkam; Sanaga Maritime and Wouri. The said units will be headed by an assistant chief of service and 10 agents for each unit except Wouri that will count 20 agents. One statistician for each subunit and one for the unit will be in charge of data collection and treatment.

For the Center region:

The Center region will be constituted by the following sub-directors:

4. The Center customs sub directorate in charge of Air surveillance (Center Zone D): It will be headed by a sub director who must have an experience of at least 05 years as customs officers. He will be assisted by chiefs of services in charge of importations by air; exportations by air; parcels and mails operations.

The chief of service of importations by air will be in charge of the following subunits and missions: surveillance of terminals, boarding of planes, controls of goods removals, delivering outing certificates, and management of customs warehouses located in the airport as well as control of all forms of passengers trafficking in collaboration with other relevant units. It will comprise in addition to the head of unit, 30 customs agents trained in air surveillance methods i.e. 05 per unit plus 01 statistician and 01 IT expert.

The chief of service of exportations by air will be in charge of the following subunits and missions: surveillance of terminals, boarding of planes, controls of goods handling, delivering relevant export customs certificates in collaboration with competent units, management of customs warehouses located in the airport as well as control of all forms of trafficking in collaboration with other relevant units. It will comprise in addition to the head of unit, 18 customs agents trained in air surveillance methods i.e. 03 per unit plus 01 statistician and 01 IT expert.

The chief of service of parcels and mails operations will be in charge of the following subunits and missions: controls of goods handling, delivering relevant export customs certificates in collaboration with competent units, It will comprise in addition to the head of unit, 06 customs agents trained in parcels and mails methods i.e. 02 per unit plus 01 statistician and 01 IT expert.

5. The Center customs sub directorate in charge of Land surveillance (Center Zone E): It will be headed by a sub director who must have an experience of at least 05 years as customs officers. He will be assisted by chiefs of services, each in charge of each administrative subdivision of the Center region i.e. Haute Sanaga; Lekié; Mbam et Inoubou; Mbam et Kim; Méfou et Afamba; Méfou et Akono; Mfoundi; Nyong et kellé; Nyong et Foumou ainsi que Nyong et So'o. The said units will be headed by an assistant chief of service and 05 agents for each unit except Mfoundi that will count 15 agents. One statistician for each subunit and one for the unit will be in charge of data collection and treatment.

- For the South region:

6. The South customs sub directorate in charge of sea surveillance (South Zone F): It will be headed by a sub director who must have an experience of at least 05 years as customs officers. He will be assisted by chiefs of services in charge of exportations by sea; imported vehicles by containers; imported vehicles not in containers; imported goods by container ; imported goods not in containers.

The chief of service of exportations by sea will be in charge of the following subunits and missions: controls of goods handling, delivering relevant export customs certificates in collaboration with competent units, management of customs warehouses located in the seaport as well as control of all forms of trafficking in collaboration with other relevant units. It will comprise in addition to the head of unit, 20 customs agents trained in sea operations surveillance methods i.e. 05 per units plus 01 statistician and 01 IT expert.

The chief of service of imported vehicles by container will be in charge of the following subunits and missions: surveillance of terminals, boarding of boats, controls of goods handling, delivering relevant customs certificates in collaboration with competent units, management of customs warehouses as well as control of all forms of trafficking in collaboration with other relevant units. It will comprise in addition to the head of unit, 18 customs agents trained in sea operations surveillance methods i.e. 03 per units plus 01 statistician and 01 IT expert.

The chief of service of imported vehicles not by container will be in charge of the following subunits and missions: surveillance of terminals, boarding of boats, controls of goods handling, delivering relevant customs certificates in collaboration with competent units, management of customs warehouses as well as control of all forms of trafficking in collaboration with other relevant units. It will comprise in addition to the head of unit, 18 customs agents trained in sea operations surveillance methods i.e. 03 per units plus 01 statistician and 01 IT expert.

The chief of service of other imported goods by container will be in charge of the following subunits and missions: surveillance of terminals, boarding of boats, controls of goods handling, delivering relevant customs certificates in collaboration with competent units, management of customs warehouses as well as control of all forms of trafficking in collaboration with other relevant units. It will comprise in addition to the head of unit, 18 customs agents trained in sea operations surveillance methods i.e. 03 per units plus 01 statistician and 01 IT expert.

The chief of service of imported goods not in containers will be in charge of the following subunits and missions: surveillance of terminals, boarding of boats, controls of goods handling, delivering relevant customs certificates in collaboration with competent units, management of customs warehouses as well as control of all forms of trafficking in collaboration with other relevant units. It will comprise in addition to the head of unit, 18 customs agents trained in sea operations surveillance methods i.e. 03 per units plus 01 statistician and 01 IT expert.

7. The South customs sub directorate in charge of land surveillance (South Zone G): It will be headed by a sub director who must have an experience of at least 05 years as customs officers. He will be assisted by chiefs of services, each in charge of each administrative subdivision of the littoral region i.e. Dja-et-Lobo ; Mvila ; Ocean and Ntem. The said units will be headed by an assistant chief of service and 10 agents for each unit except Ocean that will count 20 agents. One statistician for each subunit and one for the unit will be in charge of data collection and treatment.

- For the North region:

8. The North customs sub directorate in charge of air surveillance (North Zone H): It will be headed by a sub director who must have an experience of at least 05 years as customs officers. He will be assisted by chiefs of services in charge of importations by air; exportations by air; parcels and mails operations.

The chief of service of importations by air will be in charge of the following subunits and missions: surveillance of terminals, boarding of planes, controls of goods removals, delivering outing certificates, and management of customs warehouses located in the airport as well as control of all forms of passengers trafficking in collaboration with other relevant units. It will comprise in addition to the head of unit, 12 customs agents trained in air surveillance methods i.e. 02 per unit plus 01 statistician and 01 IT expert.

The chief of service of exportations by air will be in charge of the following subunits and missions: surveillance of terminals, boarding of planes, controls of goods handling, delivering relevant export customs certificates in collaboration with competent units, management of customs warehouses located in the airport as well as control of all forms of trafficking in collaboration with other relevant units. It will comprise in addition to the head of unit, 03 customs agents trained in air surveillance methods i.e. 01 per unit plus 01 statistician.

The chief of service of parcels and mails operations will be in charge of the following subunits and missions: controls of goods handling, delivering relevant export customs certificates in collaboration with competent units, it will comprise in addition to the head of unit, 02 customs agents trained in parcels and mails methods i.e. 01 per unit plus 01 statistician.

9. The North customs sub directorate in charge of land surveillance (North Zone I): It will be headed by a sub director who must have an experience of at least 05 years as customs officers. He will be assisted by chiefs of services, each in charge of each administrative subdivision of the North region i.e. Bénoué, Faro, Mayo Louti and Mayo rey. The said units will be headed by an assistant chief of service and 10 agents for each unit except Bénoué that will count 20 agents. One statistician for each subunit and one for the unit will be in charge of data collection and treatment.

For the Far-North region:

10. The Far North region customs sub directorate in charge of land surveillance (North Zone J): It will be headed by a sub director who must have an experience of at least 05 years as customs officers. He will be assisted by chiefs of services, each in charge of each administrative subdivision of the Far North region i.e. Diamaré, Logone et Chari, Mayo-Danay, Mayo Kani, Mayo-Sava, Mayo-Tsanaga. The said units will be headed by an assistant chief of service and 15 agents for each unit except Logone et Chari that will count 20 agents. One statistician for each subunit and one for the unit will be in charge of data collection and treatment.

- For the Adamawa region:

11. The Adamawa region customs sub directorate in charge of land surveillance (Adamawa Zone K): It will be headed by a sub director who must have an experience of at least 05 years as customs officers. He will be assisted by chiefs of services, each in charge of each administrative subdivision of the Adamawa region i.e. Djérem; Faro et Déo; Mayo-Banyo; Mbéré and Vina. The said units will be headed by an assistant chief of service and 10 agents for each unit except Vina that will count 15 agents. Including one statistician for each subunit and one for the unit will be in charge of data collection and treatment.

96

- For the West region:

12. The West region customs sub directorate in charge of land surveillance (West Zone L): It will be headed by a sub director who must have an experience of at least 05 years as customs officers. He will be assisted by chiefs of services, each in charge of each administrative subdivision of the West region i.e. Bamboutos; Haut-Nkam; Hauts-plateaux; Koung-Khi; Menoua; Mifi; Ndé and Noun. The said units will be headed by an assistant chief of service and 8 agents for each. One statistician for each subunit and one for the unit will be in charge of data collection and treatment.

- For the North West region:

13. The North-West region customs sub directorate in charge of land surveillance (North-West Zone M): It will be headed by a sub director who must have an experience of at least 05 years as customs officers. He will be assisted by chiefs of services, each in charge of each administrative subdivision of the North-West region i.e. Boyo; Bui; Donga –Mantung; Menchum; Mezam; Momo and Ngo-ketundja. The said units will be headed by an assistant chief of service and 10 agents for each except Mezam that will count 15 agents. One statistician for each subunit and one for the unit will be in charge of data collection and treatment.

- For the South West region:

14. The South-West region customs sub directorate in charge of land surveillance (South-West Zone N): It will be headed by a sub director who must have an experience of at least 05 years as customs officers. He will be assisted by chiefs of services, each in charge of each administrative subdivision of the South-West region i.e. Fako; Koupé-Manengouba; Lebialem; Manyu; Meme and Ndian. The said units will be headed by an assistant chief of service and 15 agents for each except Fako that will count 20 agents. One statistician for each subunit and one for the unit will be in charge of data collection and treatment.

- For the East region:

15. The East region customs sub directorate in charge of land surveillance (East Zone O): It will be headed by a sub director who must have an experience of at least 05 years as customs officers. He will be assisted by chiefs of services, each in charge of each administrative subdivision of the East region i.e. Lom et Djérem; Kadey; Boumba et Ngoko and Haut-Nyong. The said units will be headed by an assistant chief of service and 10 agents for each except Lom et Djérem that will count 15 agents. One statistician for each subunit and one for the unit will be in charge of data collection and treatment.

  ➢ The assistant regional director of statistics and performance: Under the technical coordination of the strategic director in charge of statistics and performance like the other units but the functional or administrative hierarchy of the regional director, He will be in charge of the customs revenues dashboard; accounting and centralization of customs revenues; follow up of customs revenues; recovery of customs revenues arrears, collecting and producing statistics of external trade; transmission of data to the strategic or relevant units; taking part in state treasury meetings at the regional level .He must be a statistician.
  In addition to 02 senior research officers having the rank of sub directors, having acquired a minimum of 05 years experience and having received a qualified training in statistics. He will be assisted by 03 junior research officers having the rank of chiefs of services and must be like the previous ones statisticians by training and specialization.

  ➢ Secretariat: secretaries will be in charge of answering calls, taking messages and handling correspondence, maintaining diaries and arranging appointments, typing, preparing and collating reports filing, organizing and servicing meetings (producing agendas and taking minutes), managing databases, prioritizing workloads, implementing new procedures and administrative systems liaising with relevant organizations, logging or processing bills or expenses. They must be holder of at least an HND in secretariat studies.

The following personnel will be entitled to a secretariat: General Manager (03); Directors (02); Assistant directors (01), operational sub directors (01).

➤ Drivers: They will be in charge of providing secure and timely driving services deliver or collect goods or mailings. They must be holder of a driving license and an experience of at least 02 years as professional driver. A test must be conducted by the directorate of supply and service attesting the qualifications proposed before posting the said driver to a particular service car. The author believes that recruiting drivers among customs agents might be of greater reliability.

The following personnel will be entitled to a driver and a service car: General Manager (02); Directors (01); Assistant directors (01), sub directors (01).

➤ The General Manager will also be entitled to a body guard who must be a police or a gendarmerie agent; 02 personnel as protocol service and 02 agents as private office personnel.

SECTION II: FURTHER SOLUTIONS AND PERSPECTIVES

In addition to the recommendations aforementioned, the author believes that the following measures will be of great impact in enhancing the performance of the Cameroon customs administration:

- Specialization of the customs personnel in the followings: public laws; logistics; accounting; auditing; IT; human resource; logistics and transports; management of real estates; courts practices; banking and finance; statistics; prospective; risks management; international trade; international cooperation; military and surveillance techniques; etc
- Harmonizing the personnel of the administration in a unique corps with clearly defined hierarchical grades. We can have an administration where all personnel wearing the uniform will be submitted to same rules and principles in terms of discipline;
- Mobility of personnel must be done according to objective principles: "The right person at the right place". This implies the putting in place of post duty descriptions for all positions with clearly defined criteria and an information system that is reliable;
- The information system must give information detailed about the number, the age, the sex, the educational background, the trainings, the professional experience, and the desired career, the marital and family status. This information system must go as far as

making a prospective analysis in terms of provisional management of jobs and skills in order to plan recruitment, selection of personnel and retirement planning.

- Performance measuring should be done systematically at all level on the basis of job description files and sanctions as well as mobility must take in consideration the said performance measuring in account.
- Customs agents must be trained at the regional level no more in the National School of Administration and Magistracy considering the fact that we have a regional customs department called Economic Community of Central African countries. This will enable to boost integration and development. Moreover the training of customs agents should be revisited. The author believes that courses like origins and evolutions of the customs; public speeches techniques; applied research methods;
- customs and geographical strategies; customs practices in administrative writing; techniques of customs surveillance; customs control of first line; customs controls of second line; customs control of third line; e-commerce and impact on customs transactions; risk management; control of internal financial transactions; auditing customs services; Analysis of customs laws and regulations; customs IT tools; management of customs human resource; customs ethics and deontology; collecting and treating customs data; prospective analyses of customs environment , can be added to order courses or replace others in order to create more expertise and performance because it appears that students coming out from school are not always operational and even after.
- A training plan must be adopted every year and the said plan must be objective and followed up. Recommendations made by trainees must be kept in archives and analyzed accordingly. The trainees must carefully be selected after analysis of the service needs and the knowledge received after training must be put in practice.
- Time management must be an issue of great concern in the running of customs administration as punctuality, attendance are parts and parcel of performance measuring in the organization (Aloumedjo, 2018) because as stated: "time is money".
- A career planning must be put in place to guarantee objectiveness in the mobility of the personnel of the Customs administration.
- Compensation must be done on an equitable and objective ground (Aloumedjo, 2018);
- Discretion in appointment should be objective rather than subjective in that vein based on the information system, the specialization requirements, the career plan and the job description, only competent personnel meeting the requirement would be promoted with regard to their past performance and other administrative criteria.

CONCLUSION

This study aimed at determining the link in between organizational chart and professional performance focusing on the case of the Cameroon Customs administration. The main problematic was on the importance and the mechanisms for the implementation of an efficient organization structure. The methodology used for that purpose was the concurrent triangulation design that implies converging both quantitative and qualitative data in order to better understand and answer research questions (Martens 2001). The statistics analyzed show that 75 % of the participants indicated that a clearly defined organization structure can lead to organizational performance. The outcomes of this research work have clearly revealed that all independent variables organizational charts have a direct and positive correlation and influence over the dependent variable (Organizational performance).

The benefits of this research can be identified in the theoretical, methodological and managerial domains. Theoretically the theories and concepts explored led us to the fact that organization structuring are useful for any organization that looks for performance and effective organizational culture. The limitations of the concepts and theories studied were also brought out in the sense that they did not take into consideration the case of specific contexts and organization such as African administration and realities may be due to the fact that they were for the essential carried out in the western environment wherefrom the importance of this study that intends to carry out such a study in that context. Methodologically the paper tried to mix both qualitative and quantitative analyses in order to better understand and answer the research problem. It further extended the scope of scientific methods explored in a study as it involved interviews; questionnaires; Performance tests; observations; follow up focus groups and document analysis. In managerial terms it puts at the disposal of managers in general and the customs administration of Cameroon in particular, tools to better up their organizational performance and job satisfaction in a context marked by the absence of a real policy of human resource management.

This study is alongside the article of the same author entitled: "A comparative study in between a professional football team and the Cameroon customs administration" which revealed that the Cameroon Customs Revenue will pass from $827.9 million a year to $ 4232, 7 million which represents almost half of the Cameroon State budget if only real HRM policies were implemented.

Although this research was carefully prepared, I am still aware of its limitations and shortcomings i.e. First of all, the difficult access to information, the population of the experimental group does not systematically represent the majority of workers and finally since the assessment of the pretest and post test was conducted by the author himself, it is possible to find in this study a certain degree of subjectivity.

In terms of research perspectives it is believed that the present research was not sufficiently explored and as such there is need to extend it to other Cameroonian administration which for the majority faces the same realities. It should be furthered in the context of the customs department by conceiving effectively a real organizational chart restructuring the said organization.

REFERENCES

1. Alexander Hamilton institute (1923) *Organization charts*. p. 6.
2. Amburgey, T. L., Kelly, D., & Barnett, W. P. 1993. Resetting the Clock: The Dynamics of Organizational Change and Failure. Administrative Science Quarterly, 38(1): 51-73.
3. ARTHUR J.B., (1994), Effects of human resource systems on manufacturing performance and turnover, Academy of Management Journal, vol. 37, n° 3, p. 670-687
4. Argyres, N. S. 1995. Technology Strategy, Governance Structure and Interdivisional Coordination. Journal of Economic Behavior &Organization, 28(3): 337-358.
5. Baligh, H. H., Burton, R. M., & Obel, B. 1996. Organizational consultant: Creating a usable theory for organizational design. Management Science, 42(12): 1648 - 1662.
6. Child, J., & McGrath, R. G. 2001. Organizations Unfettered: Organizational Form in an Information-Intensive Economy. Academy of Management Journal, 44(6): 1135.
7. Ethiraj, S., & Levinthal, D. 2004. Bounded Rationality and the Search for Organizational Architecture: An Evolutionary Perspective on the Design of Organizations and Their Evolvability. Administrative Science Quarterly, 49(3): 404.
8. Galunic, D. C., & Eisenhardt, K. M. 1996. The Evolution of Intracorporate Domains: Divisional charter losses in high-technology, multidivisional corporations Organization Science, 7(3): 255-283.
9. Garicano, L. 2000. Hierarchies and the Organization of Knowledge in Production. The Journal of Political Economy, 108(5): 874-904.
10. Geanakoplos, J., & Milgrom, P. 1991. A theory of hierarchies based on limited managerial attention. Journal of Japanese and International Economies, 5: 205-225.
11. Gresov, C., & Drazin, R. 1997. Equifinality: Functional Equivalence in Organization Design. Academy of Management Review, 22(2): 403-428.
12. Gulati, R., & Puranam, P. 2009. Renewal through reorganization: The Value of Inconsistencies between Formal and Informal Organization. Organization Science. 20(2): 422-440.
13. Keen, M., *Moderniser la douane : défis et stratégie de réforme de l'administration douanière*, FMI, 2003.
14. Lane et Michael, *International Supply Chain Management and Customs: Peru, a Case Study*, 2000.
15. MARCH J. G., SIMON H. A. (1958), Les Organisations, trad. par Rouchy J.-C., Paris, Dunod, 1999.
16. Mintzberg, H. 1990. The Design School: Reconsidering the Basic Premises of Strategic Management. Strategic Management Journal, 11(3): 171-195.

17. Vroom, G. 2006. Organizational design and the intensity of rivalry. Management Science, 52(11): 1689-1702.

18. Marcellin Djeuwou (2009), La corruption dans le management des ressources humaines de l'administration douanière, Afrique contemporaine N° 230, pages 55 à 67

FIGURE 1: CLASSIFICATON OF FONCTIONS IN THE CCA

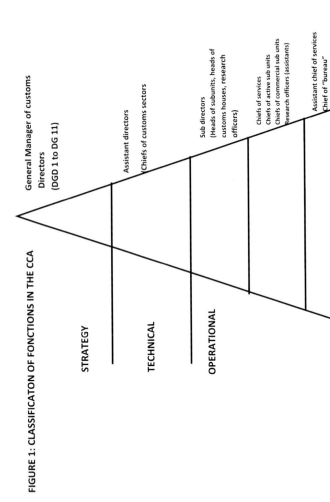

STRATEGY

General Manager of customs
Directors
(DGD 1 to DG 11)

TECHNICAL

Assistant directors
Chiefs of customs sectors

OPERATIONAL

Sub directors
(Heads of subunits, heads of customs houses, research officers)

Chiefs of services
Chiefs of active sub units
Chiefs of commercial sub units
Research officers (assistants)

Assistant chief of services
Chief of "bureau"
Customs revenue units

Additional post less staff

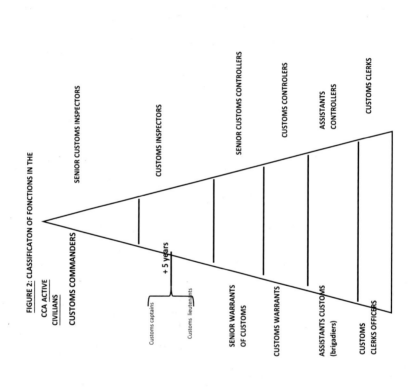

FIGURE 2: CLASSIFICATON OF FONCTIONS IN THE

CCA ACTIVE CIVILIANS

CUSTOMS COMMANDERS

SENIOR CUSTOMS INSPECTORS

CUSTOMS INSPECTORS

SENIOR CUSTOMS CONTROLLERS

CUSTOMS CONTROLERS

ASSISTANTS CONTROLLERS

CUSTOMS CLERKS

Customs captains

Customs lieutenants

+ 5 years

SENIOR WARRANTS OF CUSTOMS

CUSTOMS WARRANTS

ASSISTANTS CUSTOMS (brigadiers)

CUSTOMS CLERKS OFFICERS

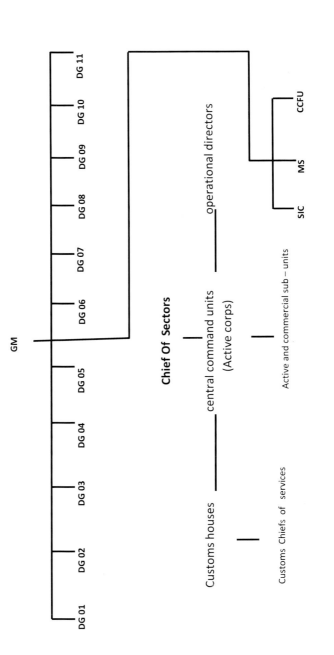

FIGURE 3 : PRESENT CHART OF THE CCA

GM

DG 01 DG 02 DG 03 DG 04 DG 05 DG 06 DG 07 DG 08 DG 09 DG 10 DG 11

Customs houses

Chief Of Sectors

central command units
(Active corps)

operational directors

Customs Chiefs of services

Active and commercial sub – units

SIC   MS   CCFU

FIGURE 4 : PROPOSED RESTRUCTURATION OF CCA

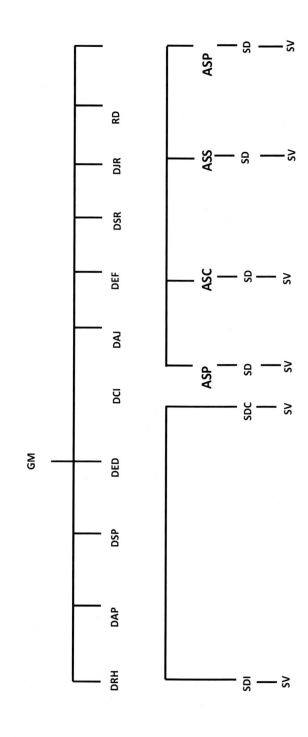

Printed by Books on Demand GmbH, Norderstedt / Germany